NEVER
TOO
LATE

FOR A NEW BEGINNING

Fountain Square   F. James McDonald

July 21, 1988

Mr. Michael Cardone, Sr.
President
M. Cardone Industries
5670 Rising Sun Avenue
Philadelphia, PA 19120

Dear Mr. Cardone:

I would consider it a great privilege to
be pictured with you in your biography. You
can be very proud of the company bearing
your name, and I am pleased to be pictured
in your book.

Best wishes and good health.

Sincerely,

F. James McDonald

F. James McDonald

Automotive Hall of Fame

DISTINGUISHED SERVICE CITATION

Presented To
MICHAEL CARDONE, SR.

In recognition of his contribution to the automotive industry through determination, dedication, knowledge and hard work.

For leadership talents, professional integrity, respect for sound principles, influencing others to believe in our industry.

For unselfish participation and contributions in civic, community, state and national programs.

February 5, 1984

CHAIRMAN OF THE BOARD

Michael Cardone, Sr. is the only *Remanufacturer* in the Automotive Aftermarket to have the distinction of being elected into the Automotive Hall of Fame. He shares this recognition with other automotive industry leaders, such as James McDonald, former President of General Motors, Henry Ford II of Ford Motor Company, Lee Iacocca of Chrysler Corporation and Carl Benz of Mercedes Benz.

Distinguished Service Citation award winners Michael Cardone, Sr. and James McDonald, President of General Motors, both recipients on February 5, 1984.

NEVER TOO LATE

FOR A NEW BEGINNING

MICHAEL CARDONE Sr.
Industrialist

Fleming H. Revell
A Division of Baker Book House Co
Grand Rapids, Michigan 49516

Unless otherwise identified, Scripture quotations in this book are taken from the King James Version of the Bible.

Scripture verses marked TLB are taken from The Living Bible, copyright © 1971 by Tyndale House Publishers, Wheaton, Illinois. Used by permission.

Some of the names in this book have been changed to protect privacy.

The author's proceeds from the sale of *Never Too Late* will go to world missions.

Library of Congress Cataloging-in-Publication Data
Cardone, Michael.
   Never too late / Michael Cardone.
     p.   cm.
   ISBN 0-8007-1603-5
   1. Cardone, Mishael.   2. Christian biography—United States.
I. Title.
BR1725.C236A3 1988
209′2′4—dc19   88-15296

Printed in the United States of America

"But seek ye first
the Kingdom of God,
and His righteousness;
and all these things
shall be added unto you.
Matthew 6:33

"As long as he
sought the Lord, God
made him to prosper."
II Chronicles 26:5

"I will instruct thee
and teach thee in the way
which thou shalt go:
I will guide thee
with mine eye."
Psalm 32:8

❧ To My Family ❧

AND THE LORD GOD SAID, 'IT ISN'T GOOD FOR MAN TO BE ALONE; I WILL MAKE A COMPANION FOR HIM, A HELPER SUITED TO HIS NEEDS.'

GENESIS 2:18 (THE LIVING BIBLE)

To my wife, Frances, my companion, my inspiration, my love. A true helpmate, she has worked so very hard. Without her I would not have made it.

Thank You, Lord.

'BUT AS FOR ME AND MY HOUSE, WE WILL SERVE THE LORD.'

JOSHUA 24:15

In appreciation to my family who serve the Lord with me: my wife Frances; my son Michael and his wife Jacquie; my dear daughter Ruth, who is now with the Lord; and my 6 beautiful grandchildren: Eric, Roger, Michael III, Christin, Ryan and Patricia; and my 3 great grandchildren.

Acknowledgments

I have been accompanied throughout my life by those of like spirit—men and women who enjoy a good challenge. To this strong and supportive nucleus of close friends, business associates, and relatives, I wish to express my gratitude:

I would like to begin by thanking the distinguished men of God who, through the years, have taught me, supported me, and most of all, prayed for me. Reverend Edward Menaldino, my Pastor and Shepherd over the past twenty years; Oral Roberts, truly a gentle man with bedrock faith; my dear friends Reverend Max Yeary and Reverend O.S. Hawkins; Dr. Thomas F. Zimmerman and Dr. G. Raymond Carlson, former and current General Superintendents of the Assemblies of God; Adrian Rogers, President of the Southern Baptist Convention, a charming and learned man; Demos Shakarian, a man whose business principles lay the foundation for many successful enterprises.

To a good friend who has strongly influenced my life with his "powerful" ministry—Dr. Norman Vincent Peale, a celebrated educator who touched my life with the *Power of Positive Thinking*.

I am grateful to my close business associates, Warren Eck, Jack Hecker, Alfred Mattarazzo, whose business acumen and friendship guided me through many ventures.

Thank you to three of my dearest friends, Judge Joseph Bruno, a compassionate jurist; Paul Putney, Esquire, my legal counsel; and Julius Cavicchia, a longtime friend.

I am grateful for my valued and long association with my Sales Reps: Walter Sullivan, Don Odom, Ray Palmaccio, Dave Sullivan, Arnie Cohen, Jack Kotter, Norm Munze, and Peter Valentine.

Thank you to the people I grew up with in Pittston: John Canonico whose contribution of colorful anecdotes and historical remembrances brought our early years to life; Nellie Daub, a warm and wonderful friend; and Josephine Barnes, Minnie Gratola, Minnie Silver, and Katie Russo.

Thank you to my brothers and sisters who walked with me down Memory Lane and helped me capture the special feelings of the wonderful childhood we enjoyed—Nick, Clara, John, Dan, Anthony, and Ruth.

To my Executive Staff at M. Cardone Industries: Mark Spuler, Peter Calo, John Tedesco, and Allan Giordano—men whose spark and drive for excellence fuels this company.

Thank you to Gale and Georgene Pettygrove—longtime employees and friends; the late Emil Fava, our first Quality

Control Engineer; and the late Jimmy Mark, our first Plant Superintendent.

My special thanks to Paul Spuler, my assistant, who worked tirelessly and relentlessly bringing volumes of disjointed thoughts and phrases together, organizing details, and caring for this project with an intensity only an author knows.

My deep gratitude to Dick Schneider, a gifted writer, who helped me put my thoughts and feelings on paper and magically captured my life with the written word.

My special thanks to the M. Cardone Industries' Factory Family—eager men and women who were, are, and will always be the cornerstone of this company.

The Bible says that children are a reward from God—my love to my son, Michael, and my daughter, Ruth—my prized possessions. And, to their spouses, Jacquie and Ruben, and my six beautiful grandchildren, Eric, Roger, Patricia, Michael III, Christin, and Ryan.

And, it goes without saying, my wife, Frances, whose love has framed my life with strength and inspiration.

Finally, all of my thanks and praise I give to God—who called me His friend, surrounded me with His faithfulness, and most of all gave me His love. I am what I am by the grace of God—to God be all the glory!

Contents

Contents

Foreword

Not too long ago a Philadelphia industrialist invited me to his city to help introduce an unusual new installation in his manufacturing plant. Some Wall Street analysts, I'm sure, would find such an installation in a business place puzzling, to say the least.

Even so, as I walked through the over-1-million-square-foot plant with its founder, Michael Cardone, I noticed happy-looking people busily operating gleaming machines producing products in demand all over the country. Clearly, Michael had followed an old formula I have espoused since I first heard it: If you wish to become a success, find a need and fill it.

Michael Cardone had found such a need—a demand for high-quality rebuilt auto parts—and now he and over 1200 co-workers were helping to fill it.

However, his success involved a lot more than producing a

product some 10 million motorists want. And it all had to do with the unusual new installation that I had been called on to dedicate that day, a chapel. That's right, a beautiful chapel in the factory where employees could pray, meditate, or just have a personal talk with the Lord.

I suppose some efficiency experts would draw back at this. "What!" I can hear one exclaiming. "Give up valuable floor space to a nonproductive facility that can't possibly add a dime of profit to your balance sheet?"

Oh, I couldn't blame him. For one cannot measure something like this in terms of unit production per square foot.

But through the years the Spirit exemplified by that chapel is what has inspired Michael Cardone, who began life as a son of an Italian-immigrant coal miner in Pennsylvania and became a leading industrialist.

Michael will tell you that it was the Lord's creative Spirit that gave him the idea for his business only eighteen years ago. Yes, it all began only eighteen years ago in the mind of a man age fifty-four, a time when many are looking forward to retirement. In fact, most people would have felt he had already earned retirement, as he had previously run a similar business successfully for thirty-five years. It was the Lord's guidance that sustained him through crises such as devastating fires, recessions, and other calamities.

It had to be a godly inspiration that led him to launch such unique employee benefit programs as seminars to help people deal with home maintenance, income-tax preparation, and other needs, classes in foreign languages, college scholarships for employees' children, Bible fellowships, full-time chaplains, and an in-plant color video system airing inspiring programs.

Michael Cardone, a sincere man of humble spirit who still doesn't mind getting his hands dirty in his factory, showed me through the plant that morning. He picked up a worn-out, greasy power-steering pump. "We get them like this, Dr. Peale," he said. Then he showed me one looking brand new and shiny, restored for service. "See, all renewed . . . kind of like what Jesus Christ does with people."

I liked his comparison. For that's exactly what the Lord can do with us. We come to Him broken down, worn, and defeated. If we give ourselves to Him, believing He will renew us, we, too, are restored for service.

And so, as with everyone who knows the story you are about to enjoy, I believe that the chapel I helped dedicate to the Lord's service that morning is the most productive part of M. Cardone Industries.

Norman Vincent Peale

A Phenomenal Happening

Recently I walked through a phenomenal happening.

I have worked in all phases of industry for almost a half century, in factories, offices, stores, and corporate headquarters. But nowhere have I ever seen a business quite like M. Cardone Industries which began as a little basement shop with a few people and within eighteen years has grown to become the largest privately owned remanufacturer of automotive parts in the nation. It is a happening because it's still growing, developing, improving.

The man behind it all is a simple, self-effacing individual who, though not of great stature, exemplifies what can happen when one turns himself completely over to God. His whole life has been guided by prayer. As a result, he has what has been called "the touch," in that just about everything he puts his hand to becomes successful.

As to the One in charge of his life, there is something meaningful about M. Cardone Industries corporate address being on Philadelphia's Rising Sun Avenue. For throughout its seventeen plants you are, indeed, reminded of the Risen Son.

For you catch God's Spirit in its buoyant atmosphere, the cheerful attitude among its twelve hundred employees who produce remanufactured auto parts renowned for their quality, dependability, and value.

You can see it in the pleasant working conditions, sense it in the family feeling generated by the numerous employee activities from self-enrichment seminars to picnics and educational classes. Walk through the plant during off-hours. Here is a group of recently arrived immigrants learning English. There is a gathering of men and women studying home-management principles. In the family fun center, a host of exuberant young people are enjoying the coinless electronic video games prior to joining in a worship service. And in one of the company's four chapels, an employee choir practices a program which will be later broadcast throughout the factory.

Inspired by their company's creed, "Excellence in all things and all things to the glory of God," M. Cardone employees strive to do their very best, fully disassembling each part that comes in, completely remanufacturing it with every element replaced or renewed, and then testing it over and over before approving it. Their insistence on quality is reflected in the many honors the industry has accorded the firm.

Founder and President, Michael Cardone, Sr., has been honored with a Distinguished Service Citation by the *Automotive Hall of Fame* which represents all phases of the auto industry. It is a recognition he received along with James

McDonald, then president of General Motors. It is an honor he also shares with other industry leaders such as Henry Ford II of Ford Motor Company, Lee Iaccoca of Chrysler Corporation, and Carl Benz of Mercedes-Benz.

In addition, he has the unique distinction of being thrice honored with the prestigious "Remanufacturer of the Year" award by the Automotive Service Industry Association. He has also been awarded with an honorary doctorate degree by Oral Roberts University.

A determined and dedicated man, Michael Cardone has to date launched five different companies: Automotive Unit Exchange (1935); M. Cardone Industries (1970); Crown Remanufacturing in conjunction with his son-in-law, Ruben Tarno (1973); ETC (Eric Tarno Carburetor Company) in association with his first grandson, Eric Tarno (1986); and Advance Remanufacturing Company with Roger Tarno, his second grandson (1988).

Most significantly, you can see the Holy Spirit at work in the generosity of this man who has tithed his profits ever since he was a little boy running three newspaper routes in his hometown of Hughestown, Pennsylvania. He tithes not only his personal income, but that of his corporation and has also established the Michael Cardone Foundation for ministries and charities. A founding regent of Oral Roberts University, he has contributed generously to a wide variety of charities and has been instrumental in developing a number of churches throughout the world. Most recently, Michael Cardone has funded the construction of an extensive Media Center at the Assemblies of God International Headquarters in Springfield, Missouri. With administrative offices, conference rooms, and a variety of studio and lab facilities, it will focus on the production of non-broadcast videos covering educational, inspirational, and motivational topics. To begin operations in 1988, the Michael Cardone Media Center will help advance worldwide communication of the Gospel.

Who is this man with the touch? How did Michael Cardone accomplish all that he has? What motivated him? Walk with him through these pages for an adventure.

Dick Schneider, Editor

NEVER TOO LATE

FOR A NEW BEGINNING

One

The Decision

A chilling November wind sighed through the bare trees lining our quiet Philadelphia suburban street. Late that night in 1969 I stared out of our living-room window pondering the question that had haunted me for months.

Should I, nearing age fifty-five, leave a secure and respected position in industry to start life over again in a risky new venture?

It was the most difficult decision I had ever faced, and again this night I had awakened from a fretful sleep. I glanced at the bedside clock; its numerals glowed 1:00 (A.M.). My wife, Frances, slept peacefully at my side. Not wanting to disturb her, I slipped on my robe and padded downstairs to the living room to think.

Thirty-five years ago I had started a little business remanufacturing vacuum-operated automotive windshield wiper motors. It was difficult getting it going; everyone predicted it would fail.

"Remanufacture windshield wipers?" laughed an acquaintance in the automobile parts business. "You're crazy, Mike, there's no market for them!"

But I learned that if one tried hard enough, one would find a market. "Find a need and fill it" is an axiom for success according to my friend, Norman Vincent Peale. And even back then I found it. There was a market for the remanufactured motors when thrifty motorists heard about them.

I worked eighteen-hour days in grubby, dirty labor. Soon I had to hire people to help me. These included my brothers, who became my partners. We expanded into remanufacturing other automobile parts. Within fifteen years Cardo Automotive had become one of the largest automotive parts remanufacturers in the nation. I became president and was looking to many more busy years when . . . .

The hall clock chimed two o'clock. I glanced up with a start. Had it been over an hour since I had come down to the living room? The night air was chill. I drew my robe around me and stepped to the window. A Thanksgiving moon was rising behind the lacelike tree branches. How fast the time had passed.

Was it really twenty-eight years ago that I met that bright-eyed, chestnut-haired girl who now slept upstairs? And our children, Ruth and Michael, Jr., shouldn't they still be toddlers? Yet Ruth was married with a family of her own, and Michael was in his last year of college.

Happily, Ruth lived nearby and we saw each other often, but how I missed Michael. For the last three years he had lived in Tulsa, Oklahoma, where he attended Oral Roberts University. We saw him only on holidays and during the summer.

As I reached for their photographs on the bookcase, the dull bronze of an object on the shelf was reflected in the moonlight and caught my heart. Reverently I picked up a small carburetor from a Briggs & Stratton two-horsepower gas engine.

Fifteen years ago I had removed it from an old lawnmower and brought it home. Together, six-year-old Michael and I sat at the kitchen table where, under my guidance, Michael carefully disassembled it, cleaned the parts, and replaced worn fittings with new ones. Finally, little fingers working ever so carefully with pliers and screwdriver, he reassembled it and proudly held it up to me, his brown eyes shining. "Better than new, Pops!"

As I stood in the dark living room, I gripped that little carburetor tightly until the metal was warm. *This* was the reason, *this* was why I stood here agonizing over my crucial decision. As Michael and I had labored together at that kitchen table, I had so long looked forward to our working together in business. Michael, I knew, shared this dream.

How many times when Michael had worked at the plant during school vacations had the two of us, striving together, tried to solve a knotty problem on the production line? How many times had we exulted in fierce joy, pounding each other on the back, when we found the answer and the line began to run smoothly again?

I wanted this joy of working together to continue for years to come. Just as King David dreamed of the day when his son, Solomon, would build the Lord's temple, I dreamed of the day when Michael would take over the business and guide it to even greater heights.

But it was not to be. My company's policy would not allow it. It was a ruling on which I had been outvoted by my partners. No one's son or daughter could rise to the firm's presidency. Management had to be shared equally among the heirs. It was a ruling that I could not and did not want to fight. According to the bylaws it was legal.

There seemed to be only one answer. Give up my presidency of Cardo, leave it, and start my own business in which Michael could join me. His graduation was only seven months away. I slumped deeper into the cushions of the sofa. Give up a business in which I had put thirty-five years of my life? Give up the income that went with it?

Pacing the carpet, shaking my head, I told myself the whole idea was ridiculous. No, no, that couldn't be the way to go. Financial security must come first, I reasoned. After all, Michael's future, I felt, was assured. He had a good head on his shoulders and would get along well in any line of business or profession he might choose. Any firm would be happy to have him.

But what would I do? Stay on at Cardo? Without my son at my side I knew that the spark driving me would die. No, I could not, did not want to stay on.

What then? The hall clock chimed three times as if to emphasize the question.

Retire? I shuddered at the thought. Working was my life. I knew that puttering in the garden, golfing, even taking trips with Frances would be interesting for only a few months. After that I would be itching to get into harness again.

Many men and women I knew rightfully enjoyed their retirement years, doing those things they had always wanted the time to do, be it a hobby, community service, or further education. God has given each of us different callings.

With me it was the thrill of developing a business, offering the world a product it needed, and, in filling that need, helping people to realize the fullest potential of the talents God had given them.

The living-room windows shuddered as the night wind became stronger, moaning mournfully through the trees.

But what kind of business could I start? And where would I get the money? I didn't have the funds needed to start a new enterprise. The thought of giving up the solid security of a good job and paycheck to step out into the cold world with nothing but my bare hands chilled me.

In a way I'd be no different from any man who loses his job. I thought of a neighbor down the street whose firm had recently been taken over by a large conglomerate. At age forty-eight he was among three hundred employees let go in a labor-reduction program. Because of his twenty-two years' service, he had been given six months' severance pay but that was little consolation to him.

"I feel like I've been fired, Mike," he groaned to me one recent afternoon when I found him raking leaves on his lawn. "Frankly, I'm so depressed I wonder if I'm fit to find another job."

I tried to encourage him and told him that he was still a young man and not to give up hope.

But as for myself, nearly fifty-five, would a bank loan me funds? Grimacing, I shook my head. No, starting over for me was just a dream. It was too late. I got up from the sofa and walked to the window again. The eastern sky was beginning to lighten.

It made sense to continue with the company I had started. Somehow, I would see out my years without Michael at my side. I yawned, stretched, and turned toward the stairs hoping to catch some sleep before daylight.

It was then as I drew my robe around me that I felt a bulge on the side. I put my hand in the pocket and discovered the little carburetor. I gripped it tightly. A deep emotion swelled within me. Michael and I *would* start a new business together. I would leave Cardo, come what may. It was *never* too late.

In fierce exultation I continued up the stairs, basking in the new freedom of my decision. Yet I felt something else, an undefinable nudging buried deep in my spirit. It was not just Michael's presence that was spurring me to start over but something else. A peculiar calling soon to be forgotten in the flush of my decision; it would return again and again in months to come.

At the top of the stairs I halted; the cold voice of the world seemed to be challenging me.

Don't be ridiculous, Mike. Starting over without funds, without even an idea of where to begin?

But as I stood there, my hand on the bannister, another voice seemed to speak in my heart: *How many times have you started over, Mike, and I have been with you all the way?*

I smiled to myself, continued on to bed, and laid down next to Frances, my mind drifting back over a half century to a little coal mining town in the eastern Pennsylvania hills, to the first time I started over.

It was a miracle.

"Points to Remember"

(1) God has given each of us a special calling: "find a need and fill it!"
(2) Take time to listen to God speaking to you.

Two

The First Miracle

The year was 1916, the place, Hughestown, Pennsylvania, on the outskirts of Pittston in the northeastern part of the state. An hysterical young mother raced up the dusty street of this little coal mining town, hugging an infant and crying, "Santa Maria Vergine!" Her panic-stricken husband ran with her, crossing himself.

To all appearances the infant was dead. It was their only remaining child. The couple had already lost three baby boys to diphtheria, a dreaded scourge as there were no antibiotics.

"No mio figlio! No mio figlio!" screamed the mother, lifting her eyes to heaven.

Her plea was not only for the mortal life of her child but for his spiritual soul. For the baby had not been baptized and everyone knew unbaptized children were not accepted into heaven.

The young parents had already been to the Catholic rectory where the priest was not available until the next day. On hearing of a Presbyterian minister who was at the other end of town on a mission assignment, the frantic couple raced to the house where he was staying.

Answering the pounding on his door, the minister saw what seemed to be a lifeless baby and heard the desperate plea, "Battesimo! Battesimo!" Nodding his understanding, he took the little bundle into his arms and ushered the parents inside.

He quickly filled a dishpan with water, blessed it, and then dipping his hand and placing it on the tiny head, said, "I baptize thee, Michael, in the name of the Father, the Son, and the Holy Ghost."

"Grazie, grazie," sighed the young mother, kissing the minister's hand. The father gratefully tried to press a worn dollar bill on the clergyman who waved it away. The couple turned and sorrowfully trudged toward their home. Now a little casket would be needed.

Then a strange thing happened.

The baby's eyelids fluttered open, bright brown eyes looked into the heavens, and a sudden healthy squall signified one thing: The child was hungry.

"Grazie, O mio Signore!" cried his mother. Hurrying into their little frame house, she quickly unbuttoned the front of her dress and the infant began taking nourishment.

I, Michael Cardone, had started over.

Hughestown was soon buzzing about the miracle. It was never clear what exactly had happened, whether I had really died or was comatose. But Mama was certain of one thing.

"God has His hand on you, Michael," she told me again and again as soon as I was able to understand. "He has something special for you to do."

Mama was rock steady in her faith in an omnipresent God who gave and took way, who punished and blessed. Papa respected Him with the same dutiful obeisance as when he lifted his hat on passing Mount Carmel Church. Papa, who daily descended hundreds of feet into the earth to swing his pick at the flintlike walls of anthracite, accepted both God and life dutifully. Joseph and Christina Cardone had immigrated to the United States from Vico del Gargano, Provincia di Foggia, a tiny village in southern Italy where life had been even harder. It had been ever thus in Italy, and they felt it would be ever thus here. Whether it was hard labor in the fields of Italy or work in the mines of America, what difference was there?

One thing was now different, however. Their son, Michael Cardone, was the only Italian boy in Hughestown who had been baptized a Presbyterian.

The determination behind that squall for nourishment remained with me as I grew up. Papa called it bravura, Mama called it foolishness. More often than not Mama was right. Perhaps it was because I was such a small boy for my age. It may have been the ravages of diphtheria. But I never grew as big as the other boys. And so I tried to make up for it.

One afternoon along the Erie Railroad tracks three eight-year-olds were playing. "Here she comes!" We strained our eyes down the rails. In the heat-shimmering distance a dark smudge was looming larger. The acrid scent of sun-baked creosote ties and hot steel rails filled the warm air as we stared in fascination at the freight locomotive thundering toward us from the Coxton yards.

The ground shook as the engine charged us, its stack snorting black smoke, piston rods flashing, driving wheels pounding. "C'mon back, Mikey, c'mon back!" screamed one of my companions who had retreated from the track.

For some reason I couldn't step back. I wanted to stay right where I was. With a roar the monster exploded past me, its whistle wailing. I was engulfed in steam and the hot smell of engine oil. Bits of grit stung my cheeks. I looked up into the face of the engineer leaning from his cab; he waved a gloved hand and I wildly signaled back.

For some minutes I stood there, the long procession of freight cars banging and clanking past, steel wheels squalling. I stared up at the swaying paint-flaked boxcars, the rusty steel sides of lurching gondolas, and drank in the names: Erie-Lackawanna, Baltimore & Ohio, Northwestern, Georgia Pacific, Milwaukee Road, Boston & Maine.

I had never been to those places. What were they like?

Finally, the red caboose flashed by leaving a sudden quiet as the freight clattered distantly around a bend. "Hey, Mikey, you stupid, why'd you stand there?" I shook my head, shrugged, joined my two friends, and we scrambled up the gravel embankment. As we walked back into town, we kicked at cans, slung stones at telephone poles, and talked of boyhood things. Yet, all the while, I was wondering where that freight train was heading.

"Hey, it's the ice man. Let's hitch a ride."

We raced to catch up with the clattering wagon, its driver hunched at the reins guiding an elderly swaybacked horse. Swinging ourselves up onto its wet, splintery wood bed, we cast a glance at the driver. He knew we were there but focused his attention on windows where housewives wanting ice delivered would post white cards turned to the twenty-five-, fifty-, seventy-five-, or one-hundred-pound chunk they needed.

We felt around the wet wood, searching for shards of crystal clear ice so good on a hot day. I leaned back, feeling the cool soak into my sweaty shirt. Gazing into the bright blue bowl of sky, my mind drifted.

"Whatcha thinking about, Mikey?" asked Frank.

"Oh, I dunno," I sighed. "How would it be if we just kept on going and never came back?"

I sat up and looked at the distant green mountains rimming our valley. "What would it be like to be anywhere but here in this little town?"

"I dunno," answered Leo, thoughtfully licking his icicle.

The longing to find out what lay beyond those mountains ached within me. I found myself resenting the small town.

H-o-o-o-t!

It was the six o'clock evening whistle of Number 9 colliery. I jumped up and swung off the wagon. I had newspapers to deliver. In fact I had three paper routes: The Scranton *Times*, the *Times Leader*, and the Wilkes-Barre *Record*.

"See you later, guys," I hollered. They waved as the wagon lumbered up the street.

Delivering papers was better than selling Cloverine Salve. That company's colorful displays in comic books showed deluxe bicycles and Daisy air rifles that "any boy or girl can easily earn by selling the highly popular Cloverine Salve to their friends and neighbors." I had sent off to the company once and received a carton of little round tins through the mail. The salve was basically petroleum jelly with a clover scent, supposedly good for everything from bee stings to hives. But in our community thrifty housewives had their own home remedies for such ailments. And as far as getting a new bicycle, I knew I'd be too old to ride it by the time I earned one.

When I got to our house I wheeled the rusty old Flyer out past the tomato plants and bean poles filling our yard. Cutting grass was one chore we didn't have. No one grew grass in Hughestown; our small plots were too precious to waste on a luxury.

Dodging our pear tree, I steered the bike around Danny, my youngest brother at the time, who was playing in the dirt with six empty sardine cans strung together with cord. To him they could have been mine cars, cargo ships, or a railroad train. I knew, I had done this myself when I was his age.

I pedaled downtown to pick up my load of papers. After folding and stuffing them into the wire basket on the bike, I followed my route, tossing the papers onto stoops and steps. I zeroed the last paper onto Mrs. Delliquanti's porch and wheeled home. The late afternoon air was fragrant with honeysuckle as my tires crunched on the gravel road. Then, there he was, Papa trudging home from his shift at Number Eight mine. He walked slowly as if he savored every minute of sunlight. He was as black as the coal he dug, day in and day out. His white teeth emerged in a smile when he saw me.

"Mikey! How you doing, son?"

"Fine, Dad." I felt sorry for my father. I knew he and Mother had come from a little town where people were so poor many of them lived in caves in the hills.

But why did he have to work so hard here? Like most of my friends' fathers, he already had that hacking, nagging cough and spit up sputum flecked with black.

And where did it get him? I remembered the longing in his eyes when he saw the 1926 Dodge touring car with yellow wood-spoked wheels a neighbor's relative drove in from New York. He never owned an automobile nor did he ever expect to.

"Son," said Papa when I asked him why he had come to

America, "we're all so much better off than in the old country. We have a chance here. You have an opportunity to do whatever you wish, to work in the mines, the silk mill. Nobody's going to tell you *how* to make your living."

My heart sank. Work in the mines? Were the men who worked in those pits any better off than the poor old mules who pulled the mine cars? Every once in a while the beasts would be brought to the surface for a respite. Almost blind from their long immersion in the Stygian darkness, cut and bruised from falling rocks and tools, they would stand in mute silence, seemingly oblivious to the sunshine and fresh air. I did not want to become like one of those mules.

Even when Mama would recall when she and Papa had given me up for dead as a baby, I questioned our circumstances.

"God has a purpose for you," said Mama.

"In the mines, Mama?"

I didn't think much about God then. He existed somewhere, I felt, but as for His paying attention to people like us in Hughestown, well, I wasn't so sure of that. I could take care of my own battles, I believed. I could stand up to a locomotive engine, I could earn money delivering newspapers, polishing shoes, working for several Hughestown stores. Somehow, someday, I was going to get out of this town.

At age thirteen, I felt I had the drive and the determination to do it. Nothing would stop me. Even the gang of older boys who hung out in front of Denardo's Grocery and Candy Store didn't bother me. Word had it they did bad things and were to be feared. But I always held my head high when I walked past them. Perhaps I was simply trying to make up for my small stature, but I wasn't about to let them think they cowed me.

One Saturday afternoon after I had shined my last pair of

shoes and was packing up my case, one of the candy store boys came and stood over me.

"What's with you?" I said, looking up from my shoeshine case.

He jerked his thumb toward his group. "C'mon."

Frightened on the inside but maintaining an air of bravado, I followed him. The leader stared me up and down and said, "We got a problem, but a smart kid like you might be able to help us."

"What is it?"

"Well, we need a couple of tools, but don't have the money. Now, old man Mertz has a lot of them in his hardware store. We can't go in there, but you work for him. We just thought a guy like you could slip in there and grab the tools we need."

I stared at him while he waited for my reaction, thumbs in his belt.

"We'll take care of you," he promised.

These big guys asking *me* to help them? A flush of pride filled me. But then I thought of what they wanted. Stealing from Mr. Mertz? He trusted me. And whenever I'd polish his shoes he'd tip me a dime.

"Naw," I shrugged.

"C'mon, Mike. You can be one of us."

The pride returned. Become one of *them*? I shifted on my feet, then said, "Tell you what, fellows, I got to go now, but how about a few days from now?"

"Sure, Mike, that'll be swell," said the leader, patting me on the shoulder.

I walked home, swinging my shoeshine case, an extra swagger in my step. I'd show those guys there was no one any better than Mike Cardone. I could do *anything*.

And then God sent Mrs. Venezia to our street.

"Points to Remember"

(1) Never underestimate the power of faith.
(2) We like to imagine we are the masters of our fate. Once we give the reins to God, the difference is immeasurable!

Three

Breakthrough on Griffith Street

It was a quiet evening, January 17, 1927, on Griffith Street. Mama, Papa, my sister Clara, three brothers, and I had just finished our supper of macaroni. Mama mentioned Mrs. Comasso who was expecting her seventh baby.

"The midwife, Mrs. Venezia, came an hour ago," said Mama, "it should be soon now."

Midwives were the rule in our town. Doctors were called only for critical emergencies. But this midwife turned out to be different.

About an hour after supper, Clara came rushing into the house. "Mama, Papa, Mrs. Venezia is standing out in the middle of the street preaching, come and hear!"

Any novelty on a cold January night was welcome and we all rushed out to see the excitement. Mrs. Venezia may have had a most difficult or easy time helping Mrs. Comasso give birth to a baby boy. But, whatever, bringing new life into the world evidently prompted her to bring new life to the neighbors. And as we, a curious group, stood around Mrs. Venezia, she began telling us about Jesus.

"God so loved the world . . . and that means you, you, and you . . . ," she began, pointing to each of us in turn, "that He sent His only beloved Son, Jesus Christ, to show us how much He cares for us." I felt Mrs. Venezia was speaking especially to me.

Her face seemed to glow as she stood under the arc light talking about Jesus. I was first attracted by her enthusiasm and then found myself becoming increasingly interested in what she had to say.

She spoke of a Promised Messiah, God's Son who came to earth to bring salvation to mankind. She portrayed Him as a real person who had walked the earth and suffered every temptation, every hardship each of us had suffered. Yet, she pointed out, with the help of God, His Father, He was able to overcome every adversity, just as He will help us overcome our difficulties.

What particularly impressed me was her saying that Jesus was right with us, all the time. All one had to do was admit he was a sinner, ask for Jesus' forgiveness, and then ask Him into his heart, promising to live as Jesus wished. The power He would give us in return, she said, would enable us to live the glorified life God has promised.

It sounded exciting, except the part about admitting I was a sinner. I had not hurt anybody, was honest, and tried to do my best at school and part-time jobs.

As Mrs. Venezia continued preaching, a woman broke down weeping, a man who lived across the street sank to his knees, and a young girl threw her arms into the air crying, "Oh, please Jesus, save me, save me!"

Then the most surprising sight occurred: Mama and Papa were kneeling, tears streaming down their faces.

One by one Mrs. Venezia stepped over to each person asking, "Do you want to receive Jesus into your heart?"

All nodded vigorously; and each committed himself to Jesus.

Kneeling before each one, she placed her hands on the person's head, and prayed for God to grant them the "baptism of the Holy Spirit."

After she had prayed for Mama and Papa, they seemed transformed and a special light glowed in their faces as they held each other close, weeping. Whatever Mama and Papa had found, I wanted it, too, and so did Clara and my brothers, Nick, John, and Danny.

As to my sins, I was beginning to realize that, admit it or not, I had them. I remembered how easy it was to tell the fellows at the candy and grocery store I'd go along and steal from Mr. Mertz. As I thought back on my thoughts and actions of the past few years, I knew I was as much of a sinner as anyone.

And so I, too, knelt down in front of Mrs. Venezia. As she placed her hands on my head, I confessed to being a sinner and asked Jesus to enter my heart.

Something happened to me then. At the time I wasn't able to articulate it. It was as if I had been given a new outlook on life. For one thing I completely dismissed what had seemed to have been an exciting offer from the boys at the candy store to join their group. *I had joined a new kind of fellowship.*

From that night on, a revival, with the same power, I'm sure, that sparked America's Great Awakening of the early eighteenth century, swept through Hughestown. Many relatives and neighbors were baptized in the Holy Spirit.

Mrs. Venezia was a member of the Assemblies of God and when her church heard how hungry we were for God's Word, they sent a minister, the Reverend Antonio Baglio, to feed us.

We started off with meetings in our home. Furniture was pushed back against the walls in our little living room to accommodate enthusiastic worshipers. Mrs. Josephine Baglio sat at the old upright piano and the lively singing could be heard to the end of Griffith Street. Brother Antonio preached from the Bible and led us in prayer together.

What struck me was the pure joy of it. We Cardones had always been a happy family, but I had not expected these meetings to be so much fun. Church, as I had previously known it, was a somber time to be endured. Now it was a time of joy, of buoyancy and spontaneity in which I actually felt the presence of Jesus Christ.

The Bible became a sought-after book that we all studied in Sunday school and in our little informal get-togethers. One of His promises made a special impression on me at that time: "In all thy ways acknowledge him, and he shall direct thy paths" (Proverbs 3:6).

"What this means, Mike," explained Brother Antonio, "is that if, in everything you think, say, or do, you listen to God and try to do what He wants, you will find that He will lead you in the right path."

"In everything?" I asked, still thinking that God was only there for the "important" things in life.

"In everything," assured Brother Antonio. "Whether you are having trouble with a test in school, or deciding what kind of work you want to do in life. Ask God for direction through His Son, Jesus Christ, and in some real way, He will guide you."

Brother Antonio was right.

Not long after our discussion I became deeply worried over an impending algebra exam. Mathematics was not one of my best subjects and I felt sure I would fail. One night I prayed, "You know I'm having a difficult time with algebra, Father," I sighed, "please show me the way."

He did, but it didn't work out in the way I thought it would.

For some reason I expected to wake up in the morning, my head brimming with algebraic equations, all memorized. Instead I found myself paying closer attention to my studies. I listened to the teacher more closely and I began to discover that algebra, instead of a dull, dry subject, was an intriguing revealment of God's logic. Instead of facing the final exam with fear, I felt a joyful confidence. Although I didn't make a perfect score, not even near perfect, I did feel as if I had advanced a light-year in my schoolwork.

When I told Brother Antonio about it, he smiled. "You know, Mike, God put the coal deep down in the earth for your father and other men to dig. He didn't leave it piled in nice pieces outside our houses to use." He tousled my hair. "If we didn't have to work for what we needed, it wouldn't mean anything to us."

I also discovered that God's guidance can be oddly direct.

During my high school years I wondered more and more about what work I would do in life. I was never drawn to the coal mines but felt guilty about it. After all, my father had supported a large family by descending into the mines day after day. If it were good enough for him, why shouldn't I follow in his footsteps? Whenever I thought about it, I prayed, "Oh Lord, please show me what to do." He did in a very real way.

Because our little church needed coal to keep the potbellied stove going, several of us volunteered to spend a day digging coal for the church. Early in the morning of my designated day I left home wondering if this were a foretaste of my life to come. Maybe, I thought, as I walked through the cool mist, I wouldn't mind the work, perhaps even like it.

After adjusting my hard hat and making sure the electric lamp attached to it worked, I stepped onto the elevator. As it rattled and shook, plummeting into the earth, rock walls rushing up past me, I felt a tightening in my stomach. Then with a jolt and clatter, it stopped and I stepped off into the mine tunnel carrying my pick. The coal wall from which I was allowed to dig was deep into the darkness. It was warm in the tunnel; heat, they told me, rose up from inside of the earth which was still molten. I had visions of Hades. I shook my head to clear it, then, standing before the coal face, raised the heavy pick and swung it down at the wall. It bounced back like I had struck steel. Anthracite *is* hard, I realized. I lifted and struck again, this time dislodging a small chunk. Again I struck, and again. Finally after a half-hour of attacking the rocklike facing, I stopped, panting, eyes smarting from sweat rolling down my face.

Five hours later I could hardly lift the pick. The small mound of coal I had dug would hardly keep our little church warm through a Sunday. But in an important way it was a profitable exercise. For through my aching bones and muscles of my small frame, God had answered my question about working in a mine: He had clearly made me for some other kind of work.

It was such down-to-earth answers to my questions that made me appreciate Brother Antonio's kind of preaching. And going to meetings at the Assemblies of God church was something all of us looked forward to, more even than the Nickelette, the five-cent-admission movie theater in Pittston.

The church was a few miles from Hughestown and a number of us, the Daileys, Silvers, De Stefanos, Camassos, Delliquantis, Canestroles, Colinos, and Alfieris would walk to Sunday morning, Sunday evening, and Tuesday evening meetings together. The walks were fun, particularly in the evening as we rollicked along, laughing, singing favorite hymns.

It was on these walks that we learned that fully accepting the Lord had its dangers, too. Others in town, including some relatives, couldn't understand what had happened to us. When people don't understand something, they may ridicule it and act suspiciously, and resentfully.

We were hit with all three.

One evening as we walked, something struck me on the shoulder. I looked at my sweater to see it covered with yellow slime and white bits of eggshell. My sister screamed as an egg struck her in the head. She was crying as she tried to rub it off her hair with her scarf. Raucous laughter broke out from the bushes flanking our path. We were beginning to learn the cost of being different.

The persecution followed us to school. "Here comes Holy Mike!" was a greeting I was becoming accustomed to whenever I stepped into class. Usually it came from a boy I'll call Mac who considered himself the class intellectual. Pointing to the Bible that I now carried along with my schoolbooks, he pushed back his blond hair and sneered, "Now don't start preaching at us, Mike, or we'll all end up rolling on the floor like you and the rest of your crazy Holy Rollers!"

Aflame with anger, I stepped forward to punch him out. Though I was small in stature, one doesn't hoe a garden and shine shoes all summer without building up some muscle.

For a moment I stood there facing Mac's jeering countenance. Then something stopped me. Maybe it was Brother

Antonio's teaching about Jesus telling us to turn the other cheek, for I stepped back. I felt so different doing this, as if something within me were dying and something bigger were taking its place. I was letting someone else handle the situation.

I lowered my fist. Mac, staring at me in puzzlement, stepped back. "Ah, g'wan," he shrugged, and turned and walked off.

From then on a new sense of peace filled me, a confidence as if I didn't have to prove myself anymore. Even the gang at the candy store didn't intimidate me. At first as I walked past their corner one of them called out, "Hey, Mike, you've forgotten something?"

"Yeah," I answered, walking on, "I've forgotten." They soon ignored me. As Brother Antonio so aptly taught: "When a man's ways please the Lord, he maketh even his enemies to be at peace with him" (Proverbs 16:7).

Yet, the new life we Cardones and others in Hughestown had found in no way hindered us from taking pleasure in the wonderful things we had previously enjoyed. Before I discovered that Jesus was a real Person, I felt that when one became "religious" one no longer could have any fun.

However, I learned that ours is not a dreary God. He created wonderful gifts for us and I found myself reveling in them even more. No longer did I feel I had to show off by standing up to the freight train.

What could be more fun than stepping out into the quiet morning cool with a pail to pick huckleberries? I felt His presence in the morning mist rising from the fields, in the jewel-like dew on the emerald leaves, and in the tart sweetness of the huckleberries that seemed to find their way to my mouth more often than the pail.

And the hozzies, oh, the hozzies. These are a wild fruit from a thorny bush and none of us knew exactly what botanical family they belonged to. The berry ripens into a deep orange glow and biting into it while rolling the fruit against one's teeth to separate the seeds is an indescribable delight. It had the piquancy of a sweet, tart fruit punch with an exotic flavor. Solomon in all his glory had never tasted anything like a hozzie! A hozzie bush was a rare find and God, I felt, surely must have made them for our pleasure.

Sometimes on these mornings when the joy of His creation especially stirred me, I found myself throwing up my arms in exultation, thanking and praising Him. Often my own words weren't sufficient for my gratefulness and the pleasure I wanted to express, and in my exuberance, syllables of a language I did not understand welled out of me. It was then I felt especially close to Him. It was all so true: "Seek ye first the kingdom of God, and his righteousness," we were told in Matthew 6:33, "and all these things shall be added unto you."

Even in experiences more mundane, such as riding the Laurel Line, I felt He was there. This was an electrified interurban trolley that wound its way between the mountains from Scranton to Wilkes-Barre. Once a year we would take it to Rocky Glen amusement park for a day of thrills on the roller coaster and Ferris wheel. The train itself was half the fun; we leaned out the windows, inhaling the fragrant aroma of the mountain laurel that gave the line its nickname.

Other joys were walking into West Pittston to the cookie factory where three cents would buy a large sack of broken cookies we'd munch as we walked past the homes of the wealthy, homes with real green lawns and luxuriant flowers. And in my new awareness of the reality of life I found myself losing any envy I once had of these privileged people and their opulent style of living.

I was finding work itself an act of praise to our Lord, whether it was delivering papers, shining shoes, or clerking at the hardware store. Even helping Mama wash clothes ceased being the chore it once was. We brothers would lift tubs of boiling water from the old coal stove and carry them into the yard where Mama cut off pieces of Fels Naphtha soap into the steaming caldron. In would go Papa's blackened mining clothes and we'd take turns stirring them with a wooden pole until the water became indigo with coal dust and Papa's clothes were again a faded blue.

But knowing Jesus brought us an even greater gift, the strength to live with the threat of mine disasters. The mine whistle was part of our everyday life. Mounted on top of the steam-generating powerhouse for No. 9 colliery, its hoarse hoot could be heard for five miles in any direction. It would blow at six in the morning as a wake-up call, again at seven to remind miners to be on their way, and finally at eight as a courtesy for housewives to set their clocks.

But the signal we feared was the two short blasts and one long screaming wail that meant a mine disaster. At its sound emergency squads, ambulances, and any man off duty would rush to the mine to give help. Mothers and wives, faces pale with anxiety, would follow to huddle in small groups, praying and waiting. It was as if the hound of hell were baying at our door; all of us would be transfixed with terror. Was Papa all right? In fearful trembling we would wait, sick with anxiety.

But after asking Jesus into our lives, His deep sustaining presence was there with us. Of course, we worried, but we also knew deep down that, no matter what happened, somehow in some way God would see us through.

In the meantime something strange was happening to me. The first time it took place was when I was playing nips with a friend. To play this game one sets a short broomstick that has been tapered on both ends like a pencil on a flat rock. The batter, using a stick, strikes the nip on one end to bounce it into the air at which moment he swings at it with his stick endeavoring to hit it out into the field. If he does, he immediately places his bat on the ground. Someone out in the field tries to catch the nip and throw it back, hoping to hit the bat which means the batter is out.

My friend, Pat, had just lifted his bat when he lowered it with a dejected sigh. "Mike," he called, "I just don't feel like it today."

I walked over to him. "What's wrong, Pat?"

"Oh, I dunno," he stammered, "but you seem to have it all together these days. You don't seem worried."

"Tell me what's wrong," I pressed.

He took his bat and began digging the ground with it. "Oh, I got problems in school. I don't think I'll get the grades to graduate this June."

"C'mon," I said, "let's sit down and talk about it." I motioned to a large flat rock on which we both settled. Pat pulled up a long piece of grass and started chewing on it. I started to pray silently, but then something told me to ask Pat to join me.

"Pat, when I'm in a bad situation, I ask the Lord for help. Do you want to pray with me?"

He nodded and I said, "Father, You know Pat's problems and how he is worried about them. You made him and know how well he can really achieve. Please help Pat understand his lessons and earn the grades he needs."

Pat was quiet for a while, and then added his own husky "Amen."

More and more young people my age came to me with their problems. I found it easy to sit down with them and talk. I also found it easy to tithe my income from my after-school jobs. Something was happening to me. More and more I began to wonder. Did God want me to become a minister, like Brother Antonio?

I had earlier felt that maybe I should become a priest or join a religious order but realized that wasn't for me. Still, I wondered, should I become a missionary? Perhaps God wanted me to go to Africa and teach those who had never heard of Jesus before.

When I asked Brother Antonio about it, he smiled and put his hand on my shoulder.

"Mike, just keep asking God for direction. He knows better than any of us what you should do. He'll guide you. It may be His will for you to become a missionary or a preacher." He looked as if something deep within him were telling him something. "Or He may want you to become a good businessman, a *Christian* businessman," he emphasized. "God knows," he added quietly, "the world needs more of them."

My wondering about my future was soon overshadowed by high school final exams. What had seemed light-years away only a short time ago was suddenly on us, graduation day.

It was a momentous event for my family for I was the first one ever to graduate from high school. Mama and Papa were so proud sitting in the audience along with my brothers and sister. And I was particularly happy when my friend, Pat, walked up to receive his diploma. As he walked down the aisle with it, he beamed proudly at me and held up his thumb and forefinger in an "OK" sign.

As to my future, I was still undecided. In trying to make up my mind, I went to Maranatha Bible School in Green Lane, Pennsylvania, for six months. But I was still no closer to a decision. In the meantime some of my friends went to work in the mines and others got jobs at the silk mill. My earlier experience in the mine had convinced me that I would not last long down there. And what was happening to Papa's deteriorating health confirmed it.

It was then Brother Antonio's advice came to mind again. "You have to step out in faith, Mike. Keep praying for guidance. Don't expect God to show you the end of the road, just the next step ahead. If you take that step in faith, He will show you the next one and the next. But *you* have to make the first move."

For some time I had a feeling that something was awaiting me in Philadelphia, but what? I had no job offer there, not even a hint of anything promising. Mama's mother, my grandmother, lived there. But who leaves home on the basis of something like that?

It was then I realized that God had put the thought of Philadelphia in my heart. I knew it was up to me to take that first step.

Just making that decision seemed to set wheels in motion. An uncle announced that his brother-in-law, John Canonico, who lived in Philadelphia, would be making a truck delivery in town soon.

"Will he be driving back to Philadelphia?" I asked.

"Sure," he smiled. "Want to go with him?"

And so the morning came when I stood at our front door with an old ragged suitcase, holding a brown paper sack of pepper-and-egg sandwiches Mama had made for the trip. I did not want that truck to come.

At 10 o'clock, just when my uncle said it would, the truck chugged up. I turned and kissed Mama, Papa, my brothers, and my sister. We were all crying. Finally, wiping away my tears, I climbed up in the seat next to my uncle's brother-in-law.

Mr. Canonico was a big friendly man with a strong handshake. He was also a discerning man who knew how badly I was feeling.

He put the truck into gear, accelerated, and I looked back waving at my family. I watched all the familiar landmarks slip past: the Mertz hardware store, the corner where I had shined shoes, the coal colliery, the crossing signal of the Laurel Line. And then we were on Route 611, pounding east on the 120-mile trip to Philadelphia.

As we headed for the mountains, Mr. Canonico said, "Never look back, Mike. Never believe that the past is better than the future."

I knew he was right, but it seemed impossible at the time. To help stave off the homesick feeling, I reached into the brown paper bag for the last lunch Mama would ever make for me. While I munched the savory sandwiches, Mr. Canonico continued talking. "The past seems safe, Mike, and I know, to you, the future is a cloud. It looks formidable from a distance. But believe me, Mike," he touched my arm for a moment, "as you enter that cloud it clears."

I wondered just what kind of cloud I was entering.

"Points to Remember"

(1) When you ask Jesus to enter your life your old self and ways are replaced by Christ-like ones.
(2) Don't expect God to show you the end of the road, just the next step ahead.

Four

In Bonney's Garage

Philadelphia in 1934 was alive. People from everywhere came to the City of Brotherly Love to see its ornate civic buildings and parks, historical halls and museums, and beautiful monuments. But all I saw during my first few weeks in the city were sooty factory gates and grimy warehouse entrances.

After settling at Grandmother Maria Donato Mark's home, I spent day after day making the rounds of industrial plants, stores, and offices. In those dark depression days "No Help Wanted" signs faced me at every door and gate. At the few places that accepted my application, the man in charge would glance at my small frame and shake his head.

One was frank about it.

"Look, kid," he grunted. "We need guys with brawn around here. It's heavy work and I don't think you'd last more than half a day. Why don't you try working in a shoe store or something?"

I didn't tell him I had been to about every shoe and other kind of store in Philadelphia. I walked away wondering if I should just give up and return home. Maybe I could get some job in the mines.

"Lord," I found myself asking, "please give me some direction."

The next day Uncle Tony drove up in his 1929 De Soto to find me on a ladder washing my grandmother's windows.

"Hey, Mikey boy, come down. I've got good news," he boomed.

When I stepped off the ladder he clapped me on the shoulder. "I found a job for you!"

"Great! Where?"

Some of his enthusiasm disappeared. "Now Mikey," he cautioned, "it's not the greatest job in the world and the pay isn't that good, but . . . ," and his face brightened, "at least it's a start. C'mon, hop in," he urged, "I'll take you there."

In his De Soto we drove to a grimy looking automotive repair garage on a busy corner. Uncle Tony introduced me to its owner, Mr. Bonney.

"Here's the man I was telling you about," he said.

Mr. Bonney stared down at me, then turned to my uncle and spat tobacco juice into a corner of his garage. "Looks like he should still be in school," he grunted.

I felt my face flushing. "Listen, mister," I retorted, "I know how to work and can handle anything that comes up."

"Hmmm," he observed, "you've got a lot of spunk for a kid your size."

Sticking out a greasy hand, he said, "OK, I'll put you on. Five bucks a week, six days. OK?"

"OK," I agreed. At least it was better than the mines.

What I didn't know was that Mama had twisted Uncle Tony's arm to get me a job. I think he owed her something. But if Uncle Tony thought he was getting on Mama's good side, he had another thought coming.

His wife had a younger brother who, of all people, was Mac, the blond sophisticate who had given me such a hard time about my religion in high school. She badgered my uncle to get Mac a job.

Uncle Tony had a trucking business hauling coal from the mines to Philadelphia. It gave him an in with the highway department and he got Mac a job as a weighmaster, weighing trucks on the road.

Mama, with that uncanny discernment mothers have, found out about it. Not only was Mac's job several cuts above working in a garage, but it paid fifteen dollars a week. Within a day she was facing her brother in Philadelphia wanting to know why Mac got a better job.

But Romans 8:28, "And we know that all things work together for good to them that love God . . ." really worked out in this situation. For if I had not worked in that garage, I might have never become involved in the auto parts remanufacturing business.

It all started with a salesman, Harry Friedman, who worked with Bonney's garage. He came up to me one morning while I was repairing a tire. He watched me work the heavy tire iron around the wheel to loosen the rim. When I stopped for a moment to catch my breath, he said, "You're pretty good, kid. You got chutzpah."

He handed me a blackened greasy chunk of metal about as big as an apple. "Know what this is?" he asked.

"Sure, a windshield wiper motor," I said. "Looks pretty worn out to me."

"Think you could rebuild it?"

"I don't know," I studied it for a moment. "I could try."

"Well, here's my idea," said Harry. "I visit a lot of garages and service stations. They all have lots of these worn-out wiper motors. They'd be happy for me to take them off their hands for nothing, or just a few pennies.

"How about it," he continued, his voice rising with enthusiasm, "if I bring in these babies and you rebuild them?"

I started to answer but he broke in. "I don't mean rebuilding them one at a time," he said excitedly, "I see you doing it on a production-line basis." He began pacing the floor, his eyes on something far beyond the walls of the garage. "Maybe twenty, fifty, a hundred at a time, two hundred!"

He turned to me. "What do you say, Mike? It could be a nice little deal for all of us. I know a number of jobbers and garages that will be happy to get them. Nothing pleases a customer more than getting a rebuilt that's just as good as new for two-thirds less money."

His enthusiasm had affected me.

"Like I said, Mr. Friedman, I could try."

Later that evening I picked up the old wiper unit and studied it. In those days these were powered by pressure resulting from vacuum generated by the car engine, not like today's electrically operated wipers.

I wasn't sure I could rebuild it. I felt I had little mechanical aptitude; in fact, I couldn't even drive a car.

I sat down at a worktable, took the wiper apart, and laid out the individual parts and studied them. I knew by now that everything on this earth was subject to God's laws, whether it be His law of gravity, mathematics, or simple logic. I figured that any piece of mechanical equipment had to work in accord with these laws. To me, it was a matter of cause and effect. After figuring out how the motors worked, I searched for the part that got the most wear. It was easy to spot: the leather paddle which, in responding to intermittent air pressure, actuated the wiper blades. With a hammer I punched out the rivets holding the paddle, removed the paddle, got some new leather, cut it to shape, and riveted it back in. I cleaned and polished each part and finally reassembled the wiper motor.

It looked brand-new. I was about to set it aside to give to Mr. Friedman the next morning when something stopped me. How did I *know* it worked?

I went over to one of the cars in the garage and replaced its good wiper motor with my rebuilt, started the engine, and switched the lever. Nothing.

I removed the wiper motor and set it next to the good one on the table. Then I carefully took both of them apart comparing them. I found that I needed to replace a gasket. I remedied it, tried the wiper again, but it still didn't work. Again I disassembled it and discovered that some dirt was clogging the air inlet valve.

After reassembling it, the rebuilt—no, *remanufactured*—wiper worked perfectly. I sat in the front seat of the car watching that blade swish back and forth, feeling the glowing satisfaction of a job well done. The next morning, when I handed the wiper motor to Mr. Friedman, knowing that it worked as well as a new one was worth far more to me than the few pennies I received in payment. Since worn parts were replaced with brand-new ones and the whole unit perfected to new or better than new condition, I felt the term *remanufactured* was more correct than *rebuilt*.

From then on every minute I could spare from my regular garage duties was used in remanufacturing the vacuum wiper motors. Mr. Friedman would bring them in from everywhere,

Altoona, Pittsburgh, Reading. He brought them in bulging coat pockets, shopping bags, and cardboard cartons. One day he came in with a whole automobile trunkful.

My heart stopped. How could I handle *that* many? Then I remembered Mr. Friedman had mentioned an assembly line. As a youngster I had seen a Pathé newsreel showing how Henry Ford ran his assembly line: first came the chassis onto which men would install the motor, then the drive train, followed by the wheels and body as it moved along on a conveyor belt.

I applied the same techniques to remanufacturing the wipers. Though I had no need of a conveyor belt, I started out by sorting them into several different piles according to manufacturer. Then I disassembled and cleaned all the parts of each batch at once. It was easy remanufacturing them. I would cut out the leather diaphragms by the dozens, according to pattern.

Mr. Friedman was impressed. As he looked at the rows of gleaming motors, he was quiet for a moment. "You know, Mike," he said, rubbing his chin thoughtfully, "I wouldn't be a bit surprised if you were running a big business someday." He had a faraway look in his eyes, and for some reason I had a strange feeling that his comment might be more prophetic than casual.

The wiper motors continued coming in and going out, providing a welcome supplement to my weekly garage salary. But more than money, I was learning about drive, determination, and hard work. I was also learning the value of honesty and trust in a working partnership. I trusted Mr. Friedman and I felt he trusted me. I believed that we were both God-fearing men. Mr. Friedman's faith was inspired by Moses and the prophets, my faith by Yeshua (Jesus), the Messiah whom the prophets had foretold.

But more than Mr. Friedman and Mr. Bonney, I was learning that I had only One to whom I had to answer: God. As Romans 12:11 directs, we are not to be slothful in business but fervent in spirit, serving the Lord. Thus I worked directly for Him.

God was a hard taskmaster. There were times when I was not completely sure of the integrity of a motor I had finished remanufacturing. It would look perfect and even test out all right. But something deep within me told me there was something not right with it. It would be tempting to pass it along with the other completed motors, but with Him looking over my shoulder, I couldn't do it. Back it would go into the bin of old worn motors waiting to be remanufactured.

If I had any second thoughts about taking the more rigorous path, they were erased by a letter from home in which Mama told about some of the youths who used to hang out at the candy store corner. Several had been in trouble; two were already in the state prison.

As I held Mama's letter I knew that but for the grace of God, I might have met a similar fate. I wondered about those fellows. Some of them had listened to Mrs. Venezia who preached so enthusiastically on the street that evening a few years ago. A few had even listened to Brother Antonio's sermons.

Why hadn't the Lord found them as He had found me? And then I realized the Lord doesn't "find" us. Nor do we have to search for Him. God is there all the time waiting. All we have to do is accept Him.

And so life continued for me as a twenty-year-old working in Mr. Bonney's garage. I had a nice room at Grandmother's house, had made friends, and, of course, went to church. Some of my friends couldn't understand why I wouldn't miss Sunday morning, Sunday evening, and Wednesday evening services at the Westmoreland Assembly of God Church.

"You work so hard, Mike," said one. "Why not take it a little easy, get some recreation, recharge your batteries?"

But that's exactly what church did for me. After putting in long hours I'd find myself getting edgy, even morose. I knew that I had drifted away from Him. After two hours in His presence, listening to His Word, singing His praises, and communing with Jesus in the realm of His Holy Spirit, I felt relaxed and happy again. But I wasn't expecting the big surprise He had planned for me.

It happened one Sunday evening, when a group of us visited another Assembly of God church on the other side of town. They were having a musical. I wasn't sure I wanted to go, but having nothing else to do that evening, I went along.

I went there to play the saxophone, but from the instant the ensemble began playing in that church, I was mesmerized. It wasn't the music but the diminutive violinist.

As she played, the violin tucked under her chin, her chestnut hair catching highlights, and her soft brown eyes intent on the music sheet before her, I was transfixed. Though normally shy with girls, I lost no time making her acquaintance over refreshments following the music.

Frances Lizzi's spirit was as lovely as her appearance and that night as I rode the streetcar home, I gazed out the window, not seeing the dark Philadelphia streets, but the lovely face of the girl I had just met. I was hopelessly in love.

I found many excuses to attend her church. On our first date I took her to an ice-cream parlor where I never could remember what I had eaten, only that we had talked on and on until the proprietor began piling chairs onto empty tables around us as a hint he wanted to scrub the floor.

After our second date, a friend asked what we had done and I told him I'd taken Frances to a White Tower restaurant for hamburgers.

He stared at me wide-eyed. "And she'll still go out with you?"

"Sure, why not?"

He gave a low whistle. "She must really be in love with you."

Frances had grown up in Philadelphia and helped acquaint me with her city's museums and art galleries. However, most of our dates were going to church together and I couldn't think of a nicer place in which to get to know someone. One night as we rode home on a streetcar, I couldn't help but recall one of my mother's old sayings:

> *In an auto any girl can be happy,*
> *In a taxi she can be jolly,*
> *But the girl worthwhile*
> *Is the girl who can smile*
> *While riding home in a trolley.*

By then I had long since decided that Frances Lizzi was definitely worthwhile.

In fact, she was the kind of girl who made a young man think more seriously about his future. When I had been with Mr. Bonney a year, a cousin said that they were taking on people at the General Motors plant. I lost no time in going over there. I discovered that, of all things, this GM installation was remanufacturing automotive fuel pumps. With my experience at Bonney's I got a job.

I began working as a bench hand, but the principles of remanufacturing fuel pumps were the same ones I had learned on vacuum motor wipers and I found it easy to come up with helpful new ideas. Soon I advanced to a better position. And mindful of the God in charge of my life, I found my job even more fun. With a better salary I saved a little money and within a few months was able to buy my first car. It was a used two-door Model A Ford for which I paid twenty dollars. But it was drivable, enough so that it was usually jammed full of people when I went to church. It had the old mechanical brakes, which only affected the rear two wheels, and when I had to stop I felt sure the angels helped.

Life was full of excitement that year. With faith in God, a wonderful girl, and a good job, what else was there? My work was becoming more interesting and fulfilling every day. In fact I found myself looking forward to Monday mornings, which seemed like heresy to most people. Again I advanced, this time to manager of my work section. The next opening up the ladder was department supervisor. Our general superintendent had given me reason to expect it.

"Can you believe it, Grandmother?" I exclaimed one evening at dinner, enjoying the macaroni she prepared so well. "Your grandson is going to become a department supervisor!"

She smiled, spooned more macaroni onto my plate, and said, "Che sarà, sarà," meaning "what is to be, will be."

I smiled at her cautious attitude but three days later learned she must have had insight.

Early Monday morning while setting up my work station a friend sauntered by. "Have you heard, Mike, we have a new department supervisor?"

My head shot up. "Supervisor?" A chill went through me.

"Yeah," said Joe casually, "I understand he's the plant supervisor's cousin."

I felt sick, betrayed. All the extra work I had done, the additional hours I had put in. I could still hear my supervisor saying as he patted me on the back, "Yes, Mike, you've a real future here." What made it worse was knowing that the new man had little talent and ability. It was all politics. Crushed and broken, I felt as if God had let me down.

As Joe walked on, anger filled me. I wanted to take my hammer and smash the work on the bench. Here I had done everything I felt He wanted me to do and look what happened. That night I was still too upset to eat dinner.

Tuesday and early Wednesday passed. I did my work as if in a daze. On Wednesday evening I went to church automatically. As I walked into the hall before services started, a friend, Ralph, discerned that I was upset about something.

Walking over to me, he put his hand on my shoulder. "What's the matter, Mike?" he asked. "You look lower than a snake's toenail."

I blurted it all out, the promises, the betrayal. He listened carefully, then said, "Mike, let's sit down over here and pray about it."

He steered me over to a pew in the back of the church where we sat down together and he prayed that God would ease the hurt in my heart and help me see His plan in all of this.

"Mike, I know how badly you feel and I can understand. But there are two important lessons you can learn from this."

"What do you mean?"

"In the first place, you put your trust in the wrong person. The Bible says to put your trust in God, not man." He flipped through the pages of his New Testament and read from 1 Thessalonians 2:4, '. . . not as pleasing men, but God. . . .'

"You, me, the world, we're all fallible, Mike," he said. "And the world is going to let you down."

I knew he was right. God had led me as a young boy in Hughestown, He had brought me to Philadelphia, had seen to it that I met Frances. I could see that at GM I had begun to put my trust in the promises of man.

"Another thing, Mike."

"Yeah?"

"Have you forgiven the plant superintendent?"

I stared at my friend. Forgive someone who had double-crossed me?

"No," I said. "I suppose maybe, sometime. . . ."

"Sometime?" he broke in. "That doesn't work, Mike. For your sake and the superintendent's sake you must forgive him *now*."

"Why now?"

"Well, in the first place, God requires this of us. If His Son died on the cross to forgive our sins, don't you think you can forgive someone for breaking a promise?"

Seeing the anger in my eyes, he continued. "The quicker you forgive, the better for you and him. Otherwise the anger is going to eat into you, Mike, like acid etching metal. It will discolor your days and nights and will take over your life. And when you don't forgive another, God finds it difficult to work in your life.

"Remember what He said in Matthew 6:15: 'But if ye forgive not men their trespasses, neither will your Father forgive your trespasses.'"

I had to admit my friend had a point. Already I felt an ache in my stomach from the anger gnawing at me.

"And don't forget," Ralph continued, "the Bible tells us whatsoever we bind on earth, we bind in heaven, and whatsoever we loose on earth, we loose in heaven. So by not forgiving him, Mike, you're binding him *and* yourself."

"OK, OK," I admitted grudgingly. "I'll try, but it's difficult."

"Ask Jesus to help you."

I did. I knew I must do it for the One who on His cross asked His Father to forgive His killers because they did not know what they were doing. It was hard to do, at first. Every time I thought of the superintendent, anger welled up within me. But then I realized that it was probably a situation much like the one in which Uncle Tony's wife twisted his arm to give the weighmaster job to her brother.

As I thought about it, I could just see my superintendent sitting at home, probably eating dinner, while his wife kept after him to give his cousin the job. The supervisor did seem to be an honorable man in everything else, and I found myself sympathizing with him for going back on his word to me. He must have suffered over it. Then, to my surprise and relief, I began to feel sorry for him and what this situation must have put him through.

When I was able to forgive him, a big weight lifted from me and I began to feel better. A new lightness pervaded the atmosphere around me. Even the grass looked greener, the sun was brighter and warmer. I felt closer to God than ever before. For I realized that my hate and anger had blocked the conduit between Him and me, as dirt clogging the windshield wiper's air tube would keep the wiper blades from working. In forgiving the supervisor I had cleaned out the dirt in that connection.

In this new closeness with Him I seemed to hear a message: *You have taken an important step in your life. Now you are ready for a bigger one.*

Instinctively I knew what that bigger step was. I would start my own business remanufacturing auto parts. I had been working at night remanufacturing windshield wiper motors, a unit with which I was already well acquainted. But that was just a small, part-time thing.

The thought of making it a full-time venture frightened me. Me, just twenty-one years old, starting a business? It didn't make sense. I had little knowledge of such things, much less the money it would take. Moreover, I still had a good job with GM with a fairly good salary. Why give it all up to go into something so questionable?

And it was then that I felt His presence, as He said to me in Joshua 1:9 (TLB), "Be bold and strong! Banish fear and doubt! For remember, the Lord your God is with you wherever you go." With that assurance I made my decision.

But how would I start my own business? I had no supplies, no customers, and no place to work. Yet I knew that when God gives you the green light, you have to take that first step.

The first step was to give up my job. I asked to see the plant superintendent and when I stepped into his office I could see he was nervous. I'm sure he thought I was coming in to give him a fight about not living up to his promise.

"Mr. Letts," I began, "I have enjoyed working here but now I feel led to start off on my own."

He lifted slightly from his chair, surprise crossing his face. He shifted uncomfortably for a moment, then his shoulders slumped.

"Mike, I can't tell you how sorry I am about that job."

I put up my hands. "Please don't feel that way, Mr. Letts, I understand."

A load seemed to lift from his shoulders. A peace filled the office. He stood and offered me his hand. I took it and we shook hands warmly.

As I walked out of the plant where I had spent the last year, I realized that if I had been given that supervisor's job, I would have stayed on at GM and would not have been open to this new opportunity. It had been the same with my first job. If I had been given the "better" one as highway weighmaster, I would never have gone to Bonney's garage and learned about rebuilding auto parts.

And now, I was starting all over again, stepping out into the unknown. It was exciting and frightening.

"Points to Remember"

(1) Remembering that God is on the job with you, always do your best job.
(2) Put your trust in God, not man. Be willing to forgive your fellow workers and associates.

Five

Grandmother's Basement

T he bare light bulb swung wildly on its ceiling cord, fling-
ing crazy shadows against the cellar walls as my head
bumped it.

"Careful, Mikey," warned Grandmother as we picked our
way around the gas plate and washtubs in her basement.
"You'll have to move some things, but I think there's a place
over here by the coal bin where you can work."

Grandmother had graciously offered to let me use her
basement as a workshop in which to remanufacture vacuum windshield wiper motors. Small pieces of coal
crunched as I stepped to the place she had pointed out. Yes,
it was enough room.

Later that day after sweeping the area, I built a work-bench and hung a light over it. Then I stepped back and looked at the production facilities of Automotive Unit Exchange, the name I had given my new company.

"Oh Lord," I silently prayed, "guide me in this new work, strengthen and illuminate me so that every product that comes off this bench may be a blessing to the person who uses it. May it keep him and everyone else who rides in his car safe." Then I went to work.

I encountered a basic problem with the new business: I had to get raw materials, which meant worn-out windshield wiper motors. By this time I had lost contact with Harry Friedman who had been getting them for Bonney's garage. I was completely on my own.

I started out in my Model A and stopped at the first garage I came to. I soon found that getting old wiper units wasn't that easy.

"Naw," said the owner, looking back over his shoulder at his waste bin. "Had a couple last week but the junk man has taken them away."

"Well, will you save any more you get?" I asked. "I'll buy them from you."

His eyes lighted up.

"Sure, fellow, I will. When I get any, I'll be sure to save them."

The next service station wasn't much better. The owner went to the rear of his building, rummaged around, and returned holding one wiper unit. "This help you?"

"Yes, thanks," I said, paying him. "Be sure to save any more for me."

As I drove away I looked at my watch. Almost an hour had passed since I began my quest and only one wiper motor. At this rate Automotive Unit Exchange, or AUE as I had begun thinking of it, would never get off the ground.

Then up the road I saw an auto junkyard. As I looked at the long rows of old cars sagging side by side I felt I had seen a gold mine. On stepping into the little shack that served as the lot's office, I found the proprietor reclining in an old oak swivel chair, his feet up on the desk.

When I told him my need, he waved toward the lot. "Sure, take all you want and we'll talk business."

After getting my toolbox from the Model A, I walked into the auto graveyard, dodging ripped fenders and twisted bumpers. Among the silent hulks I stood for a moment, the sound of highway traffic muted in the distance. Somewhere a crow called and a vagrant breeze fluttered a piece of roof upholstery behind a shattered windshield of a 1932 Packard resting in the weeds.

A poignancy came over me as I looked at its rusting body, red hexagons still showing on the wheel hubs. It had once been someone's pride and joy. Some man had probably dreamed of buying this car; I imagined him saving for the down payment, that great day when he walked into the showroom and took delivery. How happy he and his family must have been taking their first ride in it. And how he must have lovingly waxed and polished it; I could sense his pain in suffering that first dent. I could envision the car's use through the years, perhaps taking that first baby home from the hospital, family vacation trips, and now it lay here rusting in the weeds.

I looked out at the hundreds of other cars covering the lot, each one representing a long forgotten dream.

How often, I thought, do we put our hearts into something like an automobile when it is not the real end of life but only an aid to living? I thought of Christ's teaching, to make sure our treasure is in heaven and not in things that moth and rust corrupt.

I opened my tool case, remembering that God put us on this earth to serve others. My job right now was to make windshield wiper motors available at a lower cost. I pulled out a pair of pliers, wrench, and screwdriver and went to work.

Within a few hours I had a bushel basket full of old vacuum wiper motors. When I carried them to the proprietor, he looked at them in surprise and then glanced up at me. I could see a canniness in his eyes as he quoted me a ridiculously high price.

I argued with him. He wouldn't budge, figuring, I suppose, that after I had done all the work in removing them, I would accept his price.

Finally, I set the bushel basket on the ground and walked away. By the time I reached my car I heard what I was expecting. "Hey, fella, wait, maybe we can make a deal?"

We did and from then on I got a price quote from junkyard proprietors *before* I removed the units. As the Model A chugged home late that afternoon, I wondered why humans want to take advantage of each other and, of course, I realized that, since the fall of Adam and Eve from the Garden of Eden, sinful practices have abounded. Not until God touches our lives do we change, do we pattern our lives after His Son, Jesus Christ.

That evening the production line of Automotive Unit Exchange went into action. Before disassembling the wiper motors, I had to soak them in a five-gallon can of solvent to dissolve the grease. Gasoline was my solvent. After cleaning a dozen wiper units, I could hear the door at the top of the basement stairs close smartly against the fumes. It was a good thing I did not smoke. Moreover, since my workshop was right next to the furnace, I'm sure the angels were protecting me.

It was easier to sell my remanufactured vacuum wipers than to find them. When automotive parts supply jobbers found they could sell them to their customers for less than a new one with a full warranty, I soon had a good number of customers in the Philadelphia area.

Along with windshield wiper motors, I found myself delivering something else. Full of the joy that the Lord had brought me, I wanted to share it with others. As someone once so aptly said, "It's like one beggar telling another beggar where he can find bread."

I learned soon enough, however, not to buttonhole someone cold by trying to "sell" him on Jesus. I got some cold stares that way. What I did learn was that in friendly conversation an opportunity would always happen.

For example, one rainy afternoon I had called on a prospect in Trenton, New Jersey. As I was writing up his order, I noticed him gazing out the rain-streaked window with a faraway look.

"Rain always makes me gloomy," he sighed.

"Why's that?" I asked.

"Oh, you know how it is when you got troubles."

"Yes, I know," I said, silently praying for the right words to say, "if troubles were dollars I'd be a millionaire."

He gave a grim laugh. "You got 'em too, huh? Funny, everybody thinks they are the only one."

"I know," I said, "but I have a friend who always helps me out with them."

He looked up at me with interest. "Wish I had someone like that." And, of course, I told him about my friend, Jesus.

In delivering my wiper motors, I would carry a carton of a dozen units on the back platform of a trolley; but as orders grew, I loaded up the back seat of my Model A for delivery.

One of my joys in delivering the units was when Frances accompanied me. By this time we had an "understanding." Most of these deliveries were our dates. After dropping off our final shipment to Harry's Auto Supply, for example, Frances and I would make an ice-cream parlor our last stop.

As the size of our orders increased, the trouble started. We first noticed it after Frances and I chugged up in front of a jobber with his order of six dozen units. After carrying the first four dozen into his place and setting them on the floor, I went back to the car for the remainder. After setting them down on the jobber's floor, I handed him my delivery slip to sign.

"Hey," he said, "this invoice is for six dozen. I have only five dozen here." He pointed to the stack on the floor. Sure enough, there were only five dozen. I looked at the jobber. I couldn't believe I had made a mistake. But there was nothing I could do. I changed his invoice to five dozen and went on to the next customer. A few days later on another delivery the same thing happened. It was clear, of course, what was happening. When I left the jobber to get the remainder of his order, he'd quickly swipe and hide some from the first batch.

Back in the car I grumbled about it to Frances. She was irate: "To think people can be this way!" We drove along in silence for a while, then Frances spoke up. "I've got an idea, Mike."

"What's that?"

"Next time *I'll* go into the store with you and watch the delivery while you go back to the car for more."

And that's what we did. I'll never forget glancing back at Frances that first time she stayed with our delivery. Her pert chin held high, there was a determined look in her bright brown eyes that would cow any man bent on cheating us. I couldn't help but think of the Scripture that tells us though we should have the heart of a dove we should have the eye of a serpent, meaning we should be wisely watchful. More than ever my heart went out to this vivacious girl with whom I wanted to spend the rest of my life.

My own family was becoming part of the picture, too. A year after I came to Philadelphia, Mama wrote that my brother, Nick, was graduating from high school. "With the depression things here are not good," she wrote. "Do you suppose you could help him find work?" I wrote back and one by one as they graduated from high school, my other three brothers, John, Dan, and Tony, came to Philadelphia as well. Each was welcomed and eventually all became partners in AUE for its volume was growing.

We had added a new line, fuel pumps. My job at General Motors had acquainted me with them and they seemed to be a logical addition to AUE's line. Moreover, the fuel pump on my car had given out and to my chagrin, I found myself paying the service station owner for a brand-new one (in the trade we call this an OEM, or an original equipment manufacturer).

In about a year AUE had outgrown Grandmother's cellar, much to her relief. "Every time I would think of those buckets of gasoline next to my furnace, I would pray to God," she sighed. "He answered my prayers by our not having fires, and now He has given me the best answer of all: You are moving to another location."

The new location was Uncle Tony's garage. It offered more room and, best of all, no stairs to lug up cases of remanufactured wiper motors and fuel pumps. It had one problem, however. Uncle Tony could not understand my commitment to God and His Son, Jesus. With him religion was more of a mechanical habit: Go to church on Sunday and holy days, and with that duty out of the way, forget about it for the rest of the week. My going to church on weeknights and twice on Sunday seemed to make him angry. Maybe subconsciously he realized he must be missing something.

Whatever, he would come into our shop, stand at my elbow

while I would be assembling a fuel pump, and practically shout at me, "Mike, a smart guy like you wasting so much time at that crazy Pentecostal church. What's the matter with you? And don't tell me you're getting something there that I'm not getting at *my* church, the church you *should* be going to."

I had heard his tirade so many times before that it went into my left ear and out the right. But this time his argument was different. As I put the fuel pump on the test rack, his tone became more confidential. "I have to tell you, Mike, there's talk in the neighborhood about that place you call a church. There's something wrong going on there."

I stiffened as I was about to put the fuel pump into its carton. "What are you talking about, Uncle Tony?"

"The people. A friend of mine went there once and he told me he never saw anything like it."

"What did he find wrong?" I asked.

"Wrong?" he fairly shouted. "Why it's sacrilegious! Those people laugh and sing and . . ." his face whitened, ". . . and they stand up and raise their arms in the air, and. . . ." He caught his breath. "You tell me that's worship?"

I fought to keep my temper under control. Then after a quick silent prayer for the right words, I said, "Yes, it *is* worship, Uncle Tony. We go to church to thank the Lord for the good things He has done for us. And knowing He loves us makes us very happy. We sing to Him in celebration and raise our hands in joy and praise."

Uncle Tony stared at me in disbelief, his lower lip trembling. And then I got, or was given, an idea.

"Look, Uncle Tony," I said quietly. "Remember when you and I went to the Philadelphia Phillies baseball game last year, the score was tied and the Phillies hit that home run?"

His face brightened. "Yeah!" he exclaimed, but then he became rigid again. "What's *that* got to do with it?"

"Everything, Uncle. Just think back. What did *you* do when that batter sent the ball into the bleachers?"

His eyes bulged, his face went white, and he couldn't say anything. For he knew as well as I that he, I, and everybody else in the stands were standing and screaming, waving our hands and stamping our feet.

"So what's more important, Uncle Tony," I called after him as he headed for the door, "cheering because some guy knocks a ball out of the park, or raising your hands in joy to God for saving your life?"

Uncle Tony never brought up the subject again. But when he found out how AUE was prospering and that I was tithing the company's profits to my church, he could hardly believe it and the criticism escalated. I suspect it was because he now felt he hadn't set the rent high enough in our lease agreement. But he didn't have to suffer long. By this time we had added carburetors and distributors to our remanufacturing line and Uncle Tony's garage was no longer large enough. We moved to a new, more expansive location.

I gained something from Uncle Tony's comments, however. In a small way I had come to know a little how those early Christians felt when they walked into the Roman Coliseum to meet the lions.

But along with times of testing, God also blesses us with beautiful golden moments. Early one evening Frances and I sat quietly on a bench in a park overlooking the beautiful Schuylkill, the river that flows into the Delaware at Philadelphia. The setting sun polished the surface of the river a glittering bronze and for a while neither of us said anything as we held hands gazing at the beautiful scene. A deep peace filled me and I thanked God for bringing us together. I knew it had to be Him, especially after realizing Frances and I may never have met. She almost grew up in Italy instead of the United States.

Shortly after she was born, her mother became quite ill and the family felt it best that she return with her child to Italy where her mother could care for her. Before she left one of her cousins, a born-again Christian, came to visit. They prayed together and Frances's mother accepted Jesus as her Savior. Not only was her spirit renewed, but she began to feel better physically. But since all of the plans had been made for the journey, she was in a quandary about what to do.

"Oh Lord," she prayed, "please give me some sign of whether or not I should go to Italy."

After her prayer Mrs. Lizzi stepped over to the crib to check on two-month-old Frances and found her with her tiny hands folded as if in prayer. To her this was a sign that she should remain in America and not long after that she was completely healed.

"So you see, Mike," said Frances, nudging me affectionately, "you wouldn't have me if it hadn't been for Mama's prayer."

That evening as we looked over the Schuylkill, I wondered if God would answer my own prayer.

And so, holding Frances's hand, I put an arm around her shoulder and asked her to marry me.

We were married on September 28, 1941, in the Italian Pentecostal Church (now Calvary Temple) that we had both been attending and the reception was at Frances's mother's house. Instead of caviar and champagne, our guests munched on ham-and-cheese sandwiches along with cookies and fruit juice but no celebration was more joyous.

When I told Frances we were going on our honeymoon in my old car, she laughed. "Are we going to deliver windshield wiper motors?" Three days was all I could take away from my work at AUE. So we headed for Washington, D.C., planning one day to drive down to the capital, another to visit it, and a day to return.

As Frances and I strolled among our national monuments hand in hand, I thought about the freedom they symbolized, freedom for which I was so grateful. Newspaper stories told of the dictator Mussolini's ever tightening grip on the Italian people along with Nazi Germany's takeovers of neighboring countries. I felt grateful to my parents for beginning a new life in the United States, making America my home, my native land.

Late in the afternoon we went to the top of the Washington National Monument, which towers above the grassy mall. As we peered out the small windows at the top, I noticed dark storm clouds gathering in the northeast. For a moment I felt fear, fear of the unknown, fear of the turbulence that seemed to be taking over the world.

And then, as I looked out over the panorama of government buildings and monuments, I was struck by the fact that the Washington Monument stood at the apex of a huge cross, a cross of which the Capitol was at the base, the Lincoln Memorial at its head, and the White House to the north and Jefferson Memorial to the south representing the spread of the arms. To me it symbolized the godly faith on which our country was founded, a faith that would strengthen all of us through the dark days ahead. As God told us in Psalms 62:7 (TLB) our "protection and success come from God alone. He is my refuge, a Rock where no enemy can reach me."

In a small way my own faith in the work to which I believed God had called me was substantiated. On our return trip home the fuel pump on our 1933 Oldsmobile failed. The service station, into which we had been able to coast, had no remanufactured one to replace it. Reluctantly, I watched the mechanic put on a new one.

A few months later the new fuel pump gave out and this time I was able to replace it with one of our AUE remanufactured models. It lasted and lasted. As I told my customers, "Good as new, probably even *better.*"

With the bombing of Pearl Harbor on December 7, 1941, those dark clouds I had sensed in Washington did overwhelm us and Automotive Unit Exchange went on a wartime production basis.

The last prewar automobile to be assembled, a Pontiac, rolled off the production line in January 1942. From then on the millions of cars on America's roads—vital to the war effort for transportation of workers to war plants, farm produce, and other vital needs—had to last for the duration. Remanufacturing their vital parts again and again was a major factor in keeping these vehicles rolling, not to mention the tremendous energy and raw materials that were saved in the process.

In the meantime Frances and I moved into a row house at 746 Garland Street in Philadelphia. I was concerned at the price: $3500. As I signed the mortgage papers, I wondered if I were biting off more than I could chew. But as with everything, we did it on faith. Again and again, God was there.

In 1942 Ruth, our first baby, was born. However, she was two months premature and at birth weighed only two pounds, twelve ounces. As I looked at that tiny human struggling for life in her incubator, I prayed that God would give her the strength to survive. He did.

Six years later Michael came along and, again, a baby of ours was in trouble. His was a breech birth and the umbilical cord was twisted around his neck seven times. We stormed heaven with our prayers and, miraculously, he survived.

Joining us in family prayers were my father and mother who had also moved to Philadelphia. "After all, son," said my mother right after they moved, "we wanted to be with our family. And besides your father's health is not good."

I looked at this dear man who had worked so hard for all of us. He smiled in his usual jovial manner but it could not hide his deep wracking cough. Often I would come upon him, hunched over, literally hacking his life out.

Why, I wondered, did men and women have to suffer so from their employment? Other industries besides coal mining allowed unsafe practices: improper ventilation for paint-spraying areas, machines without safety guards, and poor lighting, a large factor in accidents. I vowed that in any business with which I was associated the employees would have safe and comfortable working conditions.

In 1945 World War II was over and if we thought that the need for replacement parts would diminish with the resurgence of Detroit automotive production lines, we were wrong. Used cars continued to sell at a brisk pace right along with new ones and again and again we had to increase our production facilities.

Meanwhile, Automotive Unit Exchange, which we had re-named Cardo, continued to shift with the times and began re-manufacturing foreign-car parts after overseas auto makers began entering the market in the 1950s and 60s.

My own family also progressed. Frances and I continued our activities at Calvary Temple where we both taught Sunday school and I became a deacon. Together we visited the sick, launched the first graduation party for the church's young people, and initiated a senior citizens' monthly get-together.

The years rolled on bringing joy and sadness. We mourned the death of my father and then my mother, yet realized that both had graduated to a wonderful new life with our Savior.

Joy came with the marriage of Ruth to Ruben Tarno on October 31, 1964, and they have blessed us with three grandchildren. Michael married Jacqueline Martin on June 28, 1969, right after she graduated from Oral Roberts University. While he completed his senior year at ORU, she taught in the Tulsa schools.

Something had happened to Michael at ORU in addition to meeting his life partner. In high school he had not done at all well scholastically, graduating fifty-ninth out of the sixty students in his class. "Well, Dad," he had grinned wryly, "at least I wasn't last."

In college he seemed to fulfill expectations, making only a C average during his first year. But then in his sophomore year something happened. His grades shot up and when he came home on vacation breaks he seemed a changed man; there was a different light in his eyes. It wasn't until later that I learned what had really happened.

In the meantime Cardo Industries had achieved a leading role in the auto parts remanufacturing field. By 1969 it had over 700 employees and four large buildings. As president I could continue for as long as I wished, but knowing that my son would graduate in May 1970 was giving me second thoughts. Ever since he was born I dreamed of the two of us sharing a partnership in the remanufacturing business.

As Cardo's bylaws forbid any of its partners' children from assuming company leadership, the only prospect that seemed feasible was to leave Cardo and start a new business with my son. It would mean walking away from the firm that I had started and for which I had labored so hard the past thirty-five years. My partners who understood my situation had agreed to an amicable buyout.

But the decision was not all that easy. It was stepping out into the unknown at age fifty-five that really bothered me. For I could easily lose everything!

Then, after countless nights of worry, a Scripture verse came to me. I had been reading the Bible, as I always did when facing a problem, and had turned to Proverbs, which I have found to be the best common-sense guide to practical everyday living. "Commit thy works unto the Lord, and thy thoughts shall be established" (Proverbs 16:3).

What better assurance could I have?

"Points to Remember"

(1) God put us on earth to serve others; our lives should glorify God. We are blessed to bless others.

(2) Christians, like all people, experience times of testing, sadness, and worry. What a joy to be able to take all burdens and lay them before the Lord!

Six

Beginning Again

Before I made the final decision to leave my firm and start a new career, I wanted Frances's approval. She knew I had been brooding for months but I wanted to be absolutely sure that she was as enthusiastic as I about my dream.

Ever since we delivered that first order of remanufactured vacuum windshield wipers together by streetcar over thirty years ago, Frances and I had struggled together through good times and bad. The Bible says, "Who can find a virtuous woman? for her price is far above rubies" (Proverbs 31:10). And Frances certainly was that precious. I wanted to be sure we were both in agreement; after all, she would be starting over, too.

I wanted Frances's full approval despite the dire predictions of various friends and business associates. "Mike, have you lost your mind? Starting a new company at your age? You'll be out of business within a year," stated one acquaintance.

One early winter's evening after dinner I asked Fran to sit down in our den for a talk. After picking up her sewing, she sat down and began working on a dress she was making.

"Fran," I began, "I feel it's time for me to leave Cardo and begin something new; I'm not sure that that will be right now. But before I make my decision, I want your thoughts. Will you be willing to go along with me? To help, to work with me?"

I rose from my chair and began pacing the floor. "It's going to cost us my salary, our medical coverage, life insurance, *everything*."

I stopped and looked at her. "Fran, if you feel differently about it in any way, just say the word and I'll forget it."

She smiled quietly as she drew a needle through the material and bit off the thread. My heart went out to this woman who had given so much to me. Now I was asking her at age fifty-five to give up security, a regular income, and what we had looked forward to in a few years, a comfortable retirement.

"Are you *sure*, Fran?" I pressed.

She looked up from her sewing, a sparkle in her merry brown eyes. "Look," she laughed, "I came naked into this world and naked I'm going out." She smiled. "Of course, Mike, you know I'm with you."

I leaned down and kissed her. With a woman like this, a man could accomplish anything. But what was I going to accomplish? I knew that some men in my age group, forced into early retirement, had turned their hobbies into businesses.

Recent examples, as of this writing, for instance, include men I've read about, like Bob Howard, who was business office manager for Mountain Bell when he retired early at the same age as I, fifty-five. A tennis player, he put his hobby to work teaching tennis to senior men and women in his city of Scottsdale, Arizona.

Stan Singer, a successful salesperson for a paper manufacturer, due to a shifting of territories was pushed out of his job of twenty-three years at age fifty. His hobby had been running. So what did he do? He combined his hobby with his selling experience and got a top job with *Runner's World* magazine as a New York advertising representative.

Back in 1969 I didn't know about these men, of course, but I, too, was in the same boat, starting over. I couldn't put any hobbies to work since I didn't have any. Business was my hobby and what little free time I had was devoted to my church. What extra time remained was given to Oral Roberts University where I served as Founding Regent and to the Full Gospel Businessmen's Fellowship International of which I was an International Director.

I began, however, to read of men who started new careers in their same line of work. Herb Butler of White Plains, New York, had retired at age fifty-eight from his photo studio to play golf and tennis. But after three months he said he "was totally bored." I'd feel the same way. His new enterprise would find the right photographer and supplier for everything from annual reports and aerial photography to photomurals for office buildings. At age sixty-three he said he not only got fulfillment from his work but "it keeps me young."

It was stimulating to read about other men who started over in their later years. It wasn't too late for them, and I felt sure it wasn't too late for me.

One evening everything came together. It was as if God

were telling me something. Shouldn't my new business be in the same line of work, remanufacturing auto parts? Michael, Jr., was already familiar with it, having worked at Cardo after school and on vacations. He was also, at the age of eleven, the youngest person ever to graduate from the A.C. Delco Carburetor Training Course.

But what would the product be?

Other firms, including Cardo, were already handling parts like carburetors, fuel pumps, and generators. I certainly did not want to go into competition with them. No, it had to be something no one else was handling. But what?

Jesus told us in Matthew 6:33: "But seek ye first the kingdom of God, and his righteousness, and all these things shall be added unto you."

I took my question to the One in whom I had placed my life, my trust, my future. "Oh, Father," I prayed, "please guide me to the product people need, one that You know we can do best."

Every day I prayed for direction while I sifted through ideas. Though my contract at Cardo would be finished by my fifty-fifth birthday, February 8, 1970, I felt it wise to begin making plans. Fran, my daughter, Ruth, and her husband, Ruben Tarno, would get the business going so that in May when Michael, Jr., graduated from Oral Roberts University and I completed my responsibilities at Cardo, our little company would already have a running start.

Of course I did not expect the Lord to write the name of what product we should begin remanufacturing in the clouds or speak it in my ear. Guidance, I had learned, can come in many different ways. It can be an inner feeling that you sense is from Him, a verse of Scripture that speaks to the situation, or it can result from a progression of circumstances if you keep open to Him in prayer.

This time His answer came through circumstances.

A week later while I was driving down Fifth Street in a rainstorm, my windshield wipers stopped working. I pulled over to a service station and waited while the mechanic bent under the hood. Within a few minutes his head popped up.

"You need a new wiper motor."

"Can you install it now?"

"Sure," he said, turning to his shelves of replacement parts. As he took down the carton, I could see it was a brand-new wiper motor.

"I'd prefer a rebuilt," I said.

"Nah," he shrugged. "They only come new."

I flinched as he tossed my old wiper motor onto a junk pile.

As he opened the box, unwrapped the new motor, and began installing it, I wondered, was the Lord telling me something? I walked over to the junk pile, retrieved my motor, wrapped it in a piece of paper, and set it on the floor of my car.

That night I spread newspapers over our kitchen table and placed my old electric wiper motor on them. It was about the size of a grapefruit. I cleaned off the grease and took it apart. All it needed was a new bushing and bearings. I looked up at my wife who was putting away the dinner dishes.

"Fran, I think I can do it."

She leaned down and kissed me. "Mike, for thirty years I have believed you can do anything."

With a wife like Fran, a fine daughter like Ruth and her husband, Ruben, a great son like Michael and his wife, Jacquie, what more could a man want?

To do the will of God, I thought as I idly turned the worn wiper motor core in my hands. More than ever I had been feeling that urge to do something for our Lord. But what was it, I wondered, beyond starting a new business? I knew for certain that I was not supposed to become a minister. Yes, I served on the deacon board of the Calvary Temple Assembly of God in Philadelphia for the past twenty years, had supported the Assemblies of God graduate school in Springfield, Missouri, and had been named "Churchman of the Year" by my denomination.

But it seemed far more than that. I pushed back my chair; I was alone in the kitchen now. As I sat staring at the parts of the wiper motor on the table, it seemed I could hear Moses when he cried to the Lord saying, "What shall I do?" And the Lord said to Moses, "Go on! . . . and Moses did so . . ." (taken from Exodus 17:4–6).

Well, I thought, whatever it was that God wanted me to do, I knew one thing for sure: Remanufacturing electric windshield wiper motors was part of His plan for me. And I had better go on.

Soon Fran and I began hunting a location for our new business. It was a bit clumsy with me still working at Cardo, as my contract called me to be there until February 8, 1970, my fifty-fifth birthday. But I could advise Fran over the phone and when possibilities came up, I could always take an hour to rush over and look at the property.

One day while returning from looking at a piece of property we couldn't afford, which seemed to be the rule in view of our limited budget, Fran asked, "Mike, what are you going to name the new company?"

"Hmmm," I said, stopping for a traffic light, "I hadn't really thought about it."

From then on our spare moments were spent discussing possibilities, but none seemed to have the right ring. I wanted a name that would symbolize what our new business stood for: service, quality, and availability. These three values were easy to come up with, especially when remembering Jesus' teaching, "And as ye would that men should do to you, do ye also to them likewise" (Luke 6:31).

When I put myself in the shoes of the customer, I knew I would want a supplier who had my welfare at heart (*service*). I wanted a product I could trust which spelled *quality* and instead of "Sorry, it's out of stock" excuses, I wanted *availability*.

When I mentioned this to a friend he said, "Sounds A-1 to me."

"A-1 was a term I often heard used in business. I liked the sound of it and when I opened my dictionary, there it was, right on the first page: "A-1 . . . of highest quality, first-rate; as an A-1 player in A-1 condition." And thus our new company's trade name became A-1 Remanufacturing.*

When I told Fran, her eyes twinkled. "It also puts you right up at the top in the telephone book listings."

I kissed her. "Honey, what would I do without you?"

There was something else that I had to come up with, money. Fran and I had some savings, but they were a pittance to what was needed to begin our business. Besides the property, we needed equipment, tools, and enough financing to carry us through that unknown period of time before we started making a profit. Most important were the "cores." Cores in the automotive part remanufacturing business are used parts that serve as our raw material, whether they be wiper motors, carburetors, fuel pumps, and so on.

The first banker I approached smiled pleasantly when we sat down to discuss my venture. However, as I explained my plans, his smile faded. The longer I talked, the longer his face got. Finally, after shifting uncomfortably in his chair, he cleared his throat, "Er, uh, Mr. Cardone, I'm sure you will have a viable business in time, but frankly at this stage we would feel it too much of a risk to invest the sum of money you need."

---

*Around 1980 our official corporate identification became *M. Cardone Industries, Inc.* Our product line, however, continued under the identity of A-1 Remanufacturing.

When I pressed him as to what he felt was a "risk," he said something about no one ever remanufacturing wiper motors before.

"Perhaps," he added, "if you were a younger man. . . ."

"Well, sir," I sighed as I got up to put on my coat, "they didn't say that when Churchill at age sixty-four took over the leadership of Britain during World War II."

As I left that building I think I knew what Jesus meant when he advised His followers to shake the dust off their feet where they were not welcome.

Finally, after getting to know the waiting rooms of several banks rather intimately, I found a bank that felt that it wasn't too late for me; yes, Michael Cardone *had* a future despite his age.

About the same time I got the loan another need was met. Fran called one day, excitement in her voice: "Mike, I think we got something!" The address she gave, 3911 North Fifth Street, was in a terribly rundown section of Philadelphia, but its low rent fit our low budget. However, when we drove up in front of it my heart sank. It was an old three-story row house. I looked up at its rickety walls with flaking paint, gloomy windows opaque with dirt, and a sagging roof from which a section of tar paper fluttered in the wind.

"Mike, isn't it great?"

I didn't have the heart to tell Fran that Grandmother Mark's coal bin, in which I started my first business, seemed luxurious compared to this. Together we pushed open the creaking front door and stepped inside the clammy interior. My misgivings were confirmed. Its construction seemed to date back to when our forefathers signed the United States Constitution a few miles away.

As I started down the cellar stairs, I turned back to my wife. "Fran, you'd better let me check out the basement first."

I was glad I did. At the bottom of the stairs, a rat, the size of a house cat, glared at me, its eyes glinting in the light of the dusty basement bulb. Then it wheeled and scuttled into the shadows where, from the sounds, it had many companions.

After climbing back up stairs, I took Fran's hand and smiled. "Well, honey, it's a start." I smiled to myself. Again, I was starting over in a basement.

Before anything could start, however, every square inch of 3911 North Fifth Street needed a complete going over.

"After all," said Fran, slipping on gloves and an apron and covering her hair, "cleanliness is next to godliness."

All of us pitched in, Fran, Ruth, Ruben, myself, scrubbing floors and walls, polishing windows so that the sun could shine in, and launching an all-out attack on the rats until a piece of cheese could sit in the middle of the floor unmolested.

On November 1, 1969, A-1 Remanufacturing began operating. Our first staff was my wife, Frances, daughter, Ruth, son-in-law Ruben Tarno, son, Michael, Jr. (when he wasn't at school), and his lovely wife, Jacquie. Without the help of Ruben we could never have gotten started. He was a godsend and just like another son to me as we worked side by side those first years. That first morning we assembled for prayer. Standing in the middle of our "plant," on a hard-packed dirt basement floor, we held hands and dedicated our new business to the Lord.

A supply of used windshield wiper motors was on hand and we started our little assembly line, cleaning and disassembling the motors and discarding worn parts and installing new ones. Michael, who was home from school for a few days, proudly brought me the first one off the line. "Good as new, Dad," he said proudly.

I looked at the gleaming motor in my hand, remembering how each part had been carefully tested so we could guarantee it 100 percent.

"Probably better than new," I said.

Then I reluctantly returned to my office at Cardo. In the meantime I had been preparing our catalog on wiper motors so we could control inventory and customer orders. Fran had helped me with this and soon she knew as much as I about the stock.

One night as she watched me at our kitchen table struggling with invoices and statements for our new little business, she came up with another idea.

"Mike," she said, "before I took up dressmaking and designing, I had one year of bookkeeping. Why not let me help you with that?"

I was about to shake my head wearily when it seemed as if the Lord were telling me to let Fran help me out.

"OK, honey," I sighed, "it's tough trying to do all this at night. Let me help you get started."

I told Fran to get several shoe boxes and cut an opening in the front of each, marking one for "Invoices," another for "Statements," one for "Bills," and so on.

"This way you can keep everything in order," I said.

It worked. When Fran would trudge off to our accountant's office to go over our books with him, she knew just where to find everything. Later we installed a National Cash Register accounting system, which made us more professional. When Michael's wife, Jacquie, came from college, she took over most of the bookkeeping.

However, not long after we got started I got us into trouble. One day while I was at my desk at Cardo, my secretary buzzed me. "Mrs. Cardone is on the line; she says it's urgent."

I picked up the phone. Fran was almost in tears.

"What's going on, Mike?" she cried, her voice shaking. "What are you trying to do to us?"

"Calm down, honey," I soothed. "What's wrong?"

"I'll tell you what's wrong," she said. "A big truck just pulled up in front of the building with 20,000 wiper motor cores on it. The driver says they're for us. There must be some mistake!"

I slapped my forehead. Of course! I forgot to tell Fran that I had made a deal with Chrysler Corporation to buy their surplus wiper motors returned under warranty. And now the order had been delivered.

"I . . . uh . . . Fran," I stammered. "That's all right. I ordered them from Chrysler and. . . ."

The silence on the other end of the line was deadly.

"Fran . . . Fran? I'm sorry; I should have told you."

"Yes, you should have, Mike," she said resignedly. "And now tell me what we're going to do with them?"

Now I was the silent one. Twenty thousand motors stocked in those little quarters? My mind raced.

"Fran, have them brought into the building but don't pile them up in the middle of any room; the way those floors sag I'm afraid the whole shipment will end up in the basement."

"But where, Mike, where?" demanded Frances. "And hurry; the driver is standing at my desk waiting for me to sign for the shipment."

Sweat beaded my brow as I tried to think.

Finally, I said, "Stack them around the edges of the rooms. That way those old floors won't cave in."

"OK, Mike," said Fran, "but I have to tell you Ruben thinks we're making a big mistake loading up on 20,000 cores and I'm inclined to agree with him."

"All right, all right," I sighed, "what's done is done."

Fran hung up the phone and I tried to concentrate on my work. Within two minutes my secretary buzzed me again.

"Your wife, Mr. Cardone."

I picked up the phone. "What now? What now?" I asked impatiently.

"I'll tell you 'what now' Mr. Executive," said Fran. "They want to be *paid*. And do you know what the bill amounts to?"

"Well, how much?"

"Nine thousand fifty-two dollars, *that's* how much."

"Well, write out a check."

"But I only have $9500 in our checking account."

"Write it out," was all I could say.

Thus during the first week of A-1 Remanufacturing we were already broke. I couldn't help but think of Fran's joking remark when I had asked her about our starting over together. Judging from our financial situation, it looked like we both would be going out of this world naked.

But a surprise delivery of 20,000 wiper cores wasn't our real trouble. No one, it appeared, wanted to buy remanufactured windshield wiper motors. The first auto parts dealer I phoned laughed derisively.

"You crazy, Mike," he guffawed. "Me, buy remanufactured windshield wiper motors? That's a good one! Hey," he chortled, "how about remanufactured horn buttons?" I could hear his swivel chair creaking as he rocked back and forth in it laughing. He was still laughing when I quietly hung up the phone.

His reaction was dismally prophetic. I spent hours on the phone pleading with prospects. Their argument was always the same: "But we get no calls for them."

I drove hundreds of miles from one warehouse distributor to the next, to Altoona, Pittsburgh, and Trenton, New Jersey.

When I said they could sell our motors for half the price of brand-new ones, I got this typical response from a supplier.

"Look, Mike," he said, waving a cigar at his warehouse shelves. "I've got two hundred new wiper motors back there, and nobody's complaining about the price."

Blowing a cloud of blue cigar smoke, he said, "You want me to carry double inventory? Where am I going to put them?"

I turned and trudged out of the warehouse into the parking lot. A winter rain had started. I shivered, pulled up my coat collar, climbed into the car, and slumped behind the wheel. As I stared out the rain-flecked windshield at the gray sky, I wondered if the gloomy predictions of my business associates would come true. Maybe God hadn't put this dream in my heart after all. We seemed doomed at the start.

"Points to Remember"

(1) Guidance from the Lord can come in three ways: through an inner witness, through a Scripture verse, or through a set of circumstances.
(2) Believing is useless without doing what God wants you to do.

Michael Cardone, Sr., has built the largest automotive parts remanufacturing business in the world.

Cardone Industries is a family owned business. Michael Cardone, Sr. is pictured with Michael Cardone, Jr. and Michael Cardone, III.

Michael Cardone, Sr. and Michael Cardone, Jr. are greeted by President George Bush.

Michael and Frances greet Dr. Billy Graham at the Fort Lauderdale Crusade, 1987.

Dr. Norman Vincent Peale and
Mr. Michael Cardone, Sr.

Dr. Paul Yonggi Cho, Pastor of the World's Largest Church in Seoul, Korea, speaks to Cardone employees.

Dr. George Sweeting, popular author, noted Conference Speaker and Pastor Emeritus of world famous Moody Memorial Church, visits with Michael Cardone, Sr.

Michael Cardone, Sr. with the late Dr. Thomas F. Zimmerman, General Superintendent of the Assemblies of God.

Frances and Michael pictured with Dr. and Mrs. D. James Kennedy, of the Coral Ridge Presbyterian Church, Ft. Lauderdale, Florida.

Highest Medal of Honor
Bestowed Upon Michael Cardone, Sr.

Michael Cardone, Sr. was the first recipient of the General Superintendent's Medal of Honor, conferred upon him by the Executive Presbytery of the General Council of the Assemblies of God on August 9, 1989, in Indianapolis, Indiana.

The Medal of Honor is an award of the highest degree presented to outstanding members of the Assemblies of God who have distinguished themselves through meritorious service to God, the church, community and fellow citizens. Mr. Cardone was unanimously selected by the Executive Presbytery from over 18 million Assembly of God constituents worldwide.

Rev. Phillip Bongiorno, Superintendent of the
Pennsylvania District of the Assemblies of
God, presents "Churchman of the Year" award
to Michael Cardone, Sr., in 1985.

Michael Cardone, Jr. and Philadelphia Eagles Star, Reggie White,
after Reggie spoke to over 2,000 employees at a Christmas gathering.

On February 8, 1970, Michael Cardone, Sr.'s birthday, M. Cardone Industries was born at 3911 N. 5th Street, Philadelphia, PA.

Michael Cardone, Jr. tests wiper motors,
on Cardone's first production line.

Cardone Industries has experienced explosive growth since its inception.
This architectural composite shows 18 of the current 21 Plants with over
one million square feet. Of this phenomenal growth, Michael Cardone
says, "We've only just begun!"

Michael Cardone, Sr. and Jr. with their Executive Staff, 1985.

Ground breaking ceremonies for the Michael Cardone Media Center, Springfield, MO.

Michael Cardone Media Center at the Assemblies of God Headquarters, Springfield, Missouri.

Christian Life Center, founded by Michael and Frances Cardone was dedicated, debt free, in loving memory of their daughter, Ruth, on May 9, 1993. The church is located in Bensalem, Pa.

Christian Life Center Sanctuary, Interior View

Irving Cloud Publications presents Michael Cardone, Sr.
the Jobber Topics "Top Pick" Award in 1983.

Michael Cardone, Sr. is
awarded a Doctor of Laws
degree from Oral Roberts
University, 1979 with his
son, Michael, Jr., an ORU
alumnus, at his side.

Michael Cardone, Sr. joined by other family members, at ground breaking for expansion of facilities at 5660 Rising Sun Ave.

"The Cardone family has impacted so many lives for Jesus, their desire to see Him lifted up has touched my life as well as thousands of others. Michael Cardone Sr. is a perfect example of a disciple of Jesus, one who follows Him. He gives from his heart out of love, and you can see the rewards and fruit in his life."

Cheryl Prewitt Salem
Miss America 1980

A 12 x 18 foot wall mural adorns the Plant 12 Chapel depicting the many faces of Cardone's factory family, under the leadership of Jesus Christ.

Voluntary Daily Chapel Services provide inspiration
for the Cardone Factory Family.

Dr. Charles Stanley of "In Touch Ministries", speaker at a morning Chapel Service.

The Cardone Core Division Chapel, one of 6 chapels located throughout Cardone Industries.

Cardone Industries' full-time Industrial Chaplains.

**Every workday begins with an organizational group team meeting
which concludes with a Bible reading and prayer.
There are over 100 of these employee groups currently meeting every morning.**

The Spanish New Life Center, one of six churches which meet
each week in one of the Cardone Industries' chapels.

The Cardone Industries Factory Family Fun Center houses
over 70 free video games for employees and their children.

It's not unusal to find Michael Cardone, Sr. at a production line in one of the Cardone factories.

Ground breaking ceremonies for the new Distribution Center, 1984.

**Joseph Cardone,
Michael's Father**

The Cardone brothers are pictured with their father. Back Row Left to Right: Nicholas, Joseph (father), Michael. Front Row Left to Right: Daniel, John, and Tony.

**Concetta Cardone,
Michael's Mother**

**Frances and Michael Cardone
on their engagement June 1, 1941.**

**Frances and Michael
are married, September 28, 1941.**

Michael and Frances, 1943.

Michael and Frances with their children Ruth and Michael, Jr. (Passport Photo-1958)

Michael pictured with his family, from left to right:
Michael, John, Ruth, Nick, Concetta (mother), Daniel, Clara and Tony.

Michael and Frances Cardone, Sr. pictured with their children and grandchildren in 1985.

Michael and Jacquie Cardone, Jr. with their children: Christin, Michael III, and Ryan.

Michael's daughter, Ruth, pictured with her husband, Ruben, sons, Roger and Eric, and daughter Patricia in 1985.

Grandson Roger and Miriam Tarno with great grandchildren, Julie Danielle and Jeffrey Roger.

Grandson Eric and Lisa Kay Tarno with great grandson, David Brandon.

Michael and Frances celebrated their 50th Wedding Anniversary, September 28, 1991.

500 guests assemble in the Grand Ball Room of Hotel Atop the Bellevue to honor Frances and Michael at their 50th Anniversary Party.

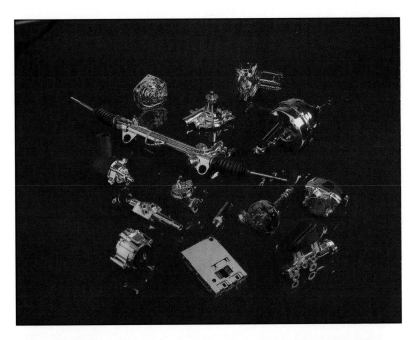

The Cardone Product Line of top quality products have been the reason why Cardone Industries is the industry's first World Class Remanufacturer. Cardone's product line includes: Engine Control Computers, Mass Airflow Sensors, Cruise Control Units, Ignition Distributors, GM PROM Chips, Master Cylinders, Power Brake Units, Disc Brake Calipers, Loaded Disc Brake Calipers, Hydro-Vac/Hydraulic Units, Rack & Pinion Units, Power Steering Pumps, Steering Gears/Control Valves, Power Cylinders, Power Steering Filters, Water Pumps, Smog Air Pumps, Wiper Motors, Window Lift Motors, Blower Motors, Radiator Cooling Motors, Tailgate Motors

Seven

Birth Pangs

As I slumped behind my steering wheel, I wondered if this was the end of our little company.

I chided myself for coming up with the electric windshield wiper motor idea. Rebuilts were successful in the vacuum wiper days but obviously not with modern electric wipers. Why hadn't I analyzed the market? What was wrong with me? I twisted in the car seat. Should we close down our little place on Fifth Street? Is this what all our work and planning had come to?

I looked up through the windshield into the gray sky and wondered. Maybe God hadn't put this dream in my heart after all. Then a word seemed to come from Him. *Think back,*

Mike, think back. I let my mind travel back to Hughestown. I remembered how God had carried me through a mortal illness as a baby, how He had walked with me, protected and guided me even when I didn't know Him.

I remembered myself as a nine-year-old, riding stomach flat on my Flexible Flyer sled down a steep icy hill into the freezing wind. I did not see the green trolley car grinding into the street crossing until it was too late. I shut my eyes, wincing at the inevitable, as I hurtled underneath the trolley. Steel wheels screamed, passengers cried out, and I slammed into something hard. Dazed, I lay motionless, afraid to open my eyes, pain searing one leg. Then men carefully eased me out from under the undercarriage and lifted me into a waiting ambulance. Miraculously, I suffered only a broken leg. Who had saved me from the steel wheels?

Of course, I knew. All through the years I had trusted Him, from my first real job at Bonney's garage to the General Motors plant where I learned so much and then on to Grandmother Mark's coal bin. He had never failed me.

I remembered those early days in Hughestown when in trouble and perplexed I would turn to Mama. She, in her earnest faith, would remind me, "God has a reason for everything, Michael, *trust Him.*"

Was I trusting Him? Wallowing in self-pity and accepting defeat was a sin. "Lord, forgive me for doubting You," I whispered as I leaned forward to turn on the ignition.

As I drove back to our little building on Fifth Street, I could almost hear Pastor Antonio talking to me again. "Remember, Michael, God put the coal in the earth but men have to dig it out. He put the oil in the rock but we have to drill for it. He gave us the wheat seeds but we have to plant, harvest, grind, and bake them to have bread. The Lord knows we need a challenge, Mike, otherwise we'd become blobs."

I felt ashamed of myself for being ready to give up. With renewed faith, I decided to start again. But this time it was with a difference. First, I put myself in the dealers' shoes, trying to understand their lack of interest. I imagined myself with the responsibility of an inventory, endeavoring to make ends meet. The enlightenment came.

Why should a dealer want to invest in a product he never had any calls for, much less heard of?

I tried a new approach on my rounds. The first prospect on my list was the heavyset cigar-smoking dealer who had shrugged me off a few days previously. When he saw me coming through his door, he blew a cloud of blue smoke and grinned. "You don't know when to give up, do you?"

"No," I smiled, "and you're going to be glad I didn't."

He leaned back in his swivel chair. "Go ahead, I've heard it all."

"Look," I said, "I'll send you some wiper motors at no risk. Make them available to your customers. See what happens when they discover they can get a good-as-new product at half the prices."

He had put down his cigar and began listening.

"Moreover," I added, "I'm going to run ads in automotive journals announcing the availability of these new remanufactured units."

I looked him straight in the eye. "Either way," I said, "you can't lose."

He stared back at me for a moment, then hoisting his ponderous bulk from the chair, he thrust out a beefy hand. "Mike, you got a deal."

Day after day I made the rounds of dealers and distributors with the same message. Not all were as enthusiastic as the first, but enough orders began coming in to keep our little business going. Our tiny production line moved slowly at first. But as more and more car owners found they could get a wiper motor at half the price of new, our little line began to hum.

Because of this, February 8, 1970, didn't come too soon for me. That was my fifty-fifth birthday, the day when I could officially join A-1 Remanufacturing as its full-time president. There was a welcoming committee to greet me on my first day at work, the entire staff of A-1, Frances, Ruth, Ruben, and Michael, Jr.

"Thank God, you're here," laughed Frances. "Now there's four of us if any of those rats show up in the basement."

In truth we had no worries about such things for with the little assembly line, core storage, and finished products lining the floors and walls of the Fifth Street premises, there wasn't room for even a mouse.

Even if one showed up, he would have had a hard time keeping out of the way of Frances, Ruth who was packing, Ruben who was handling the assembly line, and me checking finished wiper units as they came off the line. Michael would soon be with us.

Probably the busiest was Frances who turned out to be our customer relations department.

"Mom," I would hear Ruth call, "that dealer in Trenton says his order hasn't come yet and he's hopping mad."

Fran would trace the order then rush to the phone to call the dealer. But before dialing she would place both hands on the phone and shut her eyes. I knew what she was doing, praying for the dealer. Then after she called him, sure enough, everything would work out.

When I mentioned this to her later, she said, "Mike, when I awake in the morning I pray for everybody, our customers, employees, and ask our Lord to be present in our business every minute."

"Wonderful," I complimented her, not realizing that God was trying to tell me something. Unfortunately at the time I did not listen.

Fran was also our shipping department. She packed, wrapped, and when a dealer needed a wiper motor in a hurry, Fran would take it down to the post office herself to send it special delivery.

"I just want the customer to know we're trying extra hard," she said when I worried about her exerting herself too much.

But even after we shipped off the wiper motors, problems developed. "Mike," said Frances, coming up to me one day holding a motor, "this is the fifth one a customer has returned. I know these are fine when we ship them, but a gear always seems to be broken."

Were we making a mistake somewhere on the assembly line? We spent hours going over the remanufacturing process but couldn't find a bug anywhere. What was wrong?

Then I got an idea. "Fran, give me a wiper motor in its shipping container." After she handed it to me, I stood on a chair and slammed the wiper-motor carton down on the floor, just as probably happened to it in the post office. On examining it, we saw the little gear was broken. The solution was to come up with a stronger and more protective shipping container.

Often answers to what appears to be a complicated problem, I've found, come easiest when you approach it in the most uncomplicated way. But no matter how many problems we solved, or how hard we worked, it was clear to me that our little company wasn't going to make it on wiper units alone. We had to have another product. I felt it should be one that wasn't already being handled by someone else.

I studied the market, talked to dealers and garage mechanics, and found one item that seemed a good candidate: power-steering pumps. This is the unit that provides the thrust for turning the car's front wheels so that even an elderly person, hemmed in at the curb, need not worry about steering out. No one, I learned, was remanufacturing them except a Ford facility.

But when I mentioned it to others I heard a familiar refrain.

"Mike, are you crazy? There's no call for them. You'll lose your shirt. They're just too complex and too expensive to remanufacture profitably."

For guidance I turned to someone else, someone who knew the past, present, and future. "Oh Lord," I prayed, "guide us, let us know if this new product is right for us."

He answered in several ways. First, we located some good sources of power-steering pump cores. Our line was adaptable to their remanufacturing. A number of our customers expressed interest in them. Most important, everyone in A-1 Remanufacturing had a strong feeling in their hearts to go ahead.

We did and almost from the start it was obvious that adding power-steering pumps was the right move. I couldn't help but think of what the Bible said about the stone which the builders rejected: "The stone which the builders refused is become the head stone of the corner" (Psalms 118:22).

By this time our son-in-law Ruben Tarno had left us to open his own business. He had been such a wonderful help we were sorry to lose him but wished him well. (He is now president and owner of Crown Remanufacturing, Inc., which remanufactures special import lines of auto parts. His firm does such fine work that our two companies order parts from each other when special needs arise.) As more and more orders poured in we had to hire more people. Even then our employment practices were a little different from most firms. We didn't pay as much attention to the applicant's previous experience or resume as we did to the individual.

Was he or she honest? Did he or she really want to work, to advance? Ambition and the wish to do well meant more to me than any college degree. As we're told in Proverbs 26:10 (TLB): "The master may get better work from an untrained apprentice than from a skilled rebel!"

"Look," I told each new employee, "whatever we do in this place, we do for the glory of God. This means that each product that leaves this plant must be absolutely perfect. The lives of people depend on it. To have a wiper motor fail while passing a car on the highway can be deadly.

"So we work here knowing that God, the real head of our company, is looking over our shoulder, watching every move we make."

One by one new people joined us, including Mario Castillo, Jesse Dawkins, Emil Fava—and his wife, Suzy—Peter Tarnovetski, and Helene Kolbe, who was one of our first bookkeepers.

The day came when my son, Michael, came on board. We had gone to Tulsa in May 1970 to watch him graduate from Oral Roberts University. I was so very proud; he was the first person in my family to earn a university degree. Shortly afterwards, he and Jacquie moved to Philadelphia, set up housekeeping, and came to work at 3911 North Fifth Street. Jacquie, a French major, was soon typing letters on our antique Royal typewriter, but she was a good sport about it. And as I watched her working furiously, brushing blond hair from her eyes, I marveled at the way God had brought her into our family. She and Michael had come from divergent backgrounds, he from a large city and she from Fayetteville, Arkansas, where her father was a county judge and owner of a poultry processing plant.

Even when our children were small, Fran and I had prayed that the Lord would lead them to the right mate. With both Ruth and Michael, God certainly had done this.

With Michael and Jacquie it all happened so naturally. He was on the gymnastics team at ORU and Jacquie was a cheerleader. God, I believe, didn't have too much trouble bringing them together. What Michael and Jacquie did share in common from the start was a love of Jesus. She was also from a Pentecostal family, but when she told me how she had been baptized by the Holy Spirit I had tears in my eyes.

Jacquie had been traveling with ORU's World Action Singers in the Soviet Union and one night her group sang with Russian believers in a little church in Estonia.

"As we sang 'The Old Rugged Cross' together," she related, "I looked around at the earnest faces of those dear people who so bravely testified to their faith in the face of such danger and my heart seemed to burst in compassion for them. It was then I realized I was singing with them in tongues."

However, even with the Spirit of the Lord in the workplace, the world always has a way of making itself felt. A man I'll call Joe Rankor, who acted as a sort of general superintendent, opening and closing the premises, seemed to feel threatened after Michael and Jacquie arrived. One day he stormed into the office and yelled, "I quit!" That was bad enough but his wife who worked at home helped Fran out by doing some of our bookkeeping. When Joe made his announcement, he slammed the books onto a desk and left. This turned out to be Jacquie's baptism under fire for now she found herself also handling part of our bookkeeping.

She took it good-naturedly, however. "Looks like I've been promoted," she smiled as she started studying the books. Jacquie's good humor about taking on extra work typified the "one for all and all for one" spirit that pervaded our firm from the start. If someone handling a particular job suddenly needed help, there was always another person to lend a hand. If we had to work into the evening to get a big order out, everybody pitched in.

There was no false pride such as "That isn't *my* job" or "That kind of work is beneath me." Instead we worked in an atmosphere of brotherhood that helped us over the rough spots.

All in all, one could call it a family spirit. And in a way one could call Frances the "mother." No prima donna, she worked right along with the girls we hired. Come noontime, she'd take her thermos of coffee and brown paper bag lunch and sit down on a packing case with the rest of the girls. At first, one of them would rush to get her a chair.

"No, no," protested Frances, "this box is good enough."

Jesus, I felt, best spoke of the attitude that makes any family or business function well, when He said, "And whosoever will be chief among you, let him be your servant" (Matthew 20:27).

The truth of this was best illustrated after a family from Brazil took over the small living quarters that were part of our Fifth Street building. The husband began working in the plant. When Fran heard his wife was staying upstairs by herself, she said, "Send her down, I'd like to talk to her."

In a few minutes a tiny woman peered shyly around the corner of the stairs.

"Welcome, welcome," Fran greeted her. "Come over here and sit by me."

The woman slipped over to Fran and quickly sat down watching her work on some company records. With Fran's sparse Portuguese and the woman's limited English, they established communication. Soon she was helping Fran and it wasn't long before she took over some of her work. Later on she became one of our best employees who knew every part of the factory and its operation.

One day a new employee, who considered himself very much the macho man, thought he'd have some fun with her as she still looked a bit shy and retiring.

"Hi, honey," he laughed. "Can you find your way around here yet?"

The woman's eyes blazed and she drew herself up to her full height.

"What do you mean?" she snapped, pointing to Fran. "She taught me well and if you want to amount to something around here, maybe you should learn from her, too!"

The man, face blazing in embarrassment, beat a quick retreat.

The camaraderie that inspired this kind of self-assurance could only come from people working together in mutual respect. Often I found that the best way to get to know an employee was to work with him or her on the line. In fact, that's how I discovered things about my son I had never known before.

One evening we both had been working late on a tough problem involving the assembly line of power-steering pumps. Finally we called it quits and headed to our homes. Michael stopped in at our house for a late-night snack and over some of Frances's lasagna began reminiscing.

"You know, Dad," he said, "I wonder how you stood me as a kid growing up?"

"What do you mean, son?" I said, thinking of the many times I wondered the same thing myself.

"Oh, you know," he smiled. "During my early teen years our church's 'don'ts were my goals." I thought of the cigarette butts I used to find in his car.

"Yes," he said, "you probably knew I did a little smoking and drinking. And I know you and Mom knew I wasn't very happy about going to Oral Roberts University."

Michael took another bite of lasagna. "That's because I was looking for a good time at college and at ORU I figured I'd meet only long-faced guys wearing string ties and solemn girls in granny dresses carrying Bibles under their arms."

He looked up. "But all the kids I met there looked pretty sharp and everyone seemed to be having a good time. I couldn't understand it. This was supposed to be a 'religious' school. But the happier the other kids seemed to be, the more miserable I got.

"What was worse, however, were my grades," he continued. "After my miserable record in high school, I was determined to show you folks I could really make good grades. I studied my head off, but all I could come up with was a lousy C average."

I nodded, remembering my disappointment.

"Well, late in my freshman year, I was at the end of my rope. Nothing seemed to be going right. One night in my room while trying to study, I felt particularly low. Suddenly, everything seemed hopeless, my future looked bleak, and a darkness seemed to be closing in on me. With a sigh of desperation, I pushed back from my desk and I slumped in my chair. For some reason I looked up and there on my shelf was that Bible you and Mom gave me. Remember it?"

"Yes," I smiled, recalling that I felt it would never be opened.

"Well, when I saw that Bible I knew God was with me. As much as I tried to escape Him, I couldn't shake Him. I guess it was because of my church upbringing and all those altar calls I answered," he laughed. "Something must have stuck."

As I looked across the table at my son, my heart burst with gratitude, and I silently thanked God.

"So when I saw that Bible," Michael continued, "I realized that I had never really read it. Oh, sure," he grinned, "I knew by heart all the stories in it from Adam in the Garden to John writing about Armageddon. But I had never really looked into it to see what it had to say to *me*. So I reached up, took it down, and began reading the New Testament right then and there, from the start."

Michael was quiet for a moment, his thoughts seemed to be on that special moment over five years ago. "This time I really read it, Dad," he looked up, his face aglow. "I let it speak to my heart and mind. And the more I read, the more fascinated I became for in those pages I was finding the answers I had been seeking all along.

"Well, it wasn't long afterward that I felt the Lord speaking to my heart. He seemed to be saying: *If you will give your life to me, Michael, and let me control it, I will show you how to become a success."*

His voice broke as he relived that moment, then he continued. "I know God didn't mean success in money or fame, but something far deeper and more meaningful. And then He added something: *I will need some of your time, Michael; I want you to plant some seeds on behalf of others."*

Michael smiled wryly. "My first reaction was 'Hey, Lord, I've got all I can do to keep up my studies. I don't have any time.' But, Dad, His direction came again, as if He had never heard me."

My son held out his hands helplessly. "So what could I do? I had to obey Him."

Michael then told how he went to the Christian Service Counsel, an Oral Roberts University students' outreach ministry organization, serving the school and the community, and offered them his time. They put him in touch with a twelve-year-old boy who, because of a terrible home life, was practically an orphan. Would Michael become his "big brother," take him fishing, roller-skating, help him with his studies, all the things a growing boy needs?

"I was worried at first," confessed Michael. "Did I have the ability to help him? But when I met Danny, a little guy with dusty blond hair and wide blue eyes, I felt that, despite it taking vital time from my studies, this is what God wanted me to do.

"Oh, it wasn't easy," smiled Michael, remembering. "Danny was suspicious at first. The first day I went to his house to take him fishing, he stared up at me and asked, 'Why are you coming here?'

"All I could say was 'The Lord sent me.' When he finally learned I really wanted to be his friend, we had a great time together," Michael continued. "We'd pray together, thanking God for His gift of fun. Though I think praying was all new to Danny, he seemed to take to it naturally. After all, didn't the Lord say we should come unto Him as little children? In any event I feel Danny made a real commitment to Christ. Then, after about a year of our spending time together, Danny's home life improved and he went back to his mother."

Michael stared into space for a moment. "For the first time in my life, Dad, I felt as if I had done something useful for another person. It made me feel that maybe I had something to offer my fellow man."

Again he smiled in recollection. "But do you know what one of my biggest surprises was through all this? It's what happened to my time. I can't begin to explain it, but the seed I planted by working with Danny grew into a real blessing for me. You'll remember that I had worried about taking time away from my studies to help Danny? Well, just the reverse happened. For the Lord gave me new insight in how to study, He quickened my mind in assimilating facts, and He helped me understand what my professors really wanted from me. Well, before long my grades shot up and, Dad, can you believe it? I actually found myself enjoying studying."

"Yes, son," I leaned forward and clasped his shoulder, "and I also remember when you made the dean's list."

The room was still as we both sat quietly in our own thoughts. All I could think of was the truth of Joshua's statement when in speaking of families, he said, ". . . but as for me and my house, we will serve the Lord" (Joshua 24:15). *All* of my house, I believed, was now serving the Lord.

A few weeks later, I was happy to discover that Michael's education did not stop at ORU, that he was still learning. He had been reminding me how crowded we had become in our little place on Fifth Street. Cores were stacked everywhere and our little assembly lines were snaking around corners. As we worked, we were practically bumping into each other.

"Dad, we need more space," pressed Michael for seemingly the hundredth time.

"I know, son, I know," I said. Michael was right, but I had more pressing concerns on my mind and I didn't have time to think about it.

At the time I was more concerned with how Michael and Felip, one of our newer employees, were getting along together. They both worked in the same department. Felip was a middle-aged man who had come up the hard way. A tough macho type, he had little use for "college guys." And I knew that Michael had little patience with Felip. All I could do was pray and keep my eyes and ears open.

I got my answer during a talk Michael and I had after working late one night. Again we talked over a snack.

"You know, Dad," said Michael, "I had a difficult time accepting Felip. He's a rough character and I don't even think he's a Christian. In fact, I pretty well turned him off.

"Then this problem with the power-steering pump came up. A little rotor on a cam assembly was squeaking, actually causing a whining noise when we tested it. I tried and tried to figure out what was wrong, to no avail.

"Felip comes along and says he'd like to help. At first I wanted to shrug him away. I felt it was something I could remedy myself. And, frankly, I really didn't like the guy.

"But then I remembered, as we're told in Acts 10:34, God is no respecter of persons, and if He isn't, I had better not be either. And so, turning down my prejudice, I told him what the problem was. Well, you know, he picked up the power-steering pump, looked at it, felt inside the cylinder, and said, 'Michael, something seems to be a little rough on the inside where the cam wears.'

"When he said that, a light bulb went off in my head. I picked up the pump, studied it, and sure enough, inside was a small spot worn by the cam that one normally could not see. Well, there was no problem in adjusting our assembly line to take care of the situation."

Michael took a sip of his coffee. "Felip is a great asset to the company, with a natural aptitude for getting to the root of a problem. What I learned, Dad, is that no matter how much a person turns you off, you have to look deeper than a man's outside to discover the real treasure within."

It was a good thing to hear from Michael. However, it wasn't long after this little talk that I got some other news from my son that wasn't good. In fact, at the time I felt it was a disaster.

By November of 1970 Fran and I decided to take a small vacation. It had been a long time since we'd been away and we flew down to Florida for a brief respite from the cold Philadelphia winter that seemed to be coming on with a vengeance that year.

One morning after a walk on the beach, we returned to our room to find the phone ringing. I picked it up to hear Michael's voice. It was strained and broken. "Dad, we had a fire; the whole place is gone."

"Points to Remember"

(1) Although we may lapse into doubt, God has always been there and will be there for us.
(2) When we are too quick to judge others, we overlook their God-given talents.

Eight

Starting Over

"Michael, Michael, was anyone hurt?"

"No, Dad," he sobbed, "but everything's gone. We're doomed."

My son sounded so stricken my heart went out to him.

"Don't worry, son, it's all right. Mother and I will be right home."

After I put down the phone, Frances and I knelt at our bedside and prayed, holding on to the promise of Romans 8:28, ". . . all things work together for good to them that love God. . . ."

But when we got home it was difficult to trust in that promise. When we met Michael at 3911 North Fifth Street where our building had stood, the scene was utter desolation. The fire had happened on one of the coldest days in Philadelphia's history. Ice from the fire hose water covered the blackened ruins like white marble tombstones.

Michael looked desolate, too. His eyes were dark pools of fatigue in a haggard face. For the past twenty-four hours he had been searching through the charred remnants with fire inspectors and insurance adjustors.

"We don't know exactly how it started, Dad," he sighed, "but it looks like someone left a pair of greasy overalls on an electric heater after the main electrical switch had been turned off when the plant closed the night before. When the supervisor opened the plant the next morning and threw the switch, the heater glowed and set the clothes on fire."

I shook my head, not really concerned with how the fire started, but how we were going to come out of it. When we picked our way to where our little office area had been located, it hit me. All our vital records were gone. Of our bookkeeping and inventory records, plus all the cataloging I had so carefully done on our products, nothing was left but charred flakes.

An icy wind shrilled through the blackened skeleton of the building, driving the acrid smell of charred wood into my nostrils. I pulled up my coat collar and shivered. Was this the end of our dream? The thought hovered about me like a demon trying to gain entrance.

Michael and I climbed back to the sidewalk where some of our employees stood with questioning faces. Alex, a foreman, wiped his eyes, red rimmed from crying.

I took his arm. "Don't worry, Alex," I heard myself saying. "We will be back in business. We'll all be working together again." I wished I could believe my words. Was it too late to begin again?

That evening some of my old partners at Cardo phoned. All of them expressed their condolences. And all suggested that this might be a good time to reassess my situation. "Why don't you come back to Cardo?" asked my brother, Tony.

"Thanks, no," I was quick to say. "Though I appreciate the invitation."

After I hung up the phone I was surprised to find myself thinking how easy everything would be if I simply returned to Cardo. After all, I had good relationships with my former partners. I could be back at my old desk again. It would all be simple.

Then I caught myself: What was wrong with me? The Lord had brought us this far. Why wouldn't He also see us through a fire? With God, it was *never* too late. I rose from my chair with a new feeling of optimism. What had Michael been saying a week or so ago about another building being available? Something on Clear . . . Clearing . . . Clearfield, that was it. I picked up the phone and called him.

"Yes, Dad," he said, "I had mentioned it when it seemed obvious that we'd need more room."

"How big is it?"

"Oh, about two thousand square feet."

I did some quick arithmetic, my heart beating faster.

"Is it still available?"

"I don't know."

"Let's call the realtor first thing tomorrow."

I went to bed looking forward to morning. Yes, with God's help, we *were* starting over. Again.

The next day, signed lease in hand, Michael, Jacquie, Frances, and I went over and inspected the new building at 121 Clearfield, a short distance away from our old place. We would claim the premises for the Lord. I pushed open the door, reached around, felt for the light switch, and pressed the button. Big ceiling lights flooded the interior with brilliance.

We stood mouths open. The lease stated that the premises would be delivered to us "broom clean," meaning clear of any impediment. But all over the floor sat large packing crates and drums. None of us said anything for a moment. Then Michael and I looked at each other. "Perfect," we almost said in unison.

With the help of several employees, we picked up some long planks at the lumberyard and carted them to our new building. Then we arranged the packing crates and drums in rows, laid the planks across the top of them, and voilà! Perfect work tables for our assembly line! The crates and drums, you see, were waist high.

Within three days of the fire, we were back in operation. Three days. I couldn't help but think of the significance of this.

When I was a youngster and especially worried about something, such as losing one of my after-school jobs, my mother would advise me, "Wait three days."

When she first did this, I asked why.

"It's like Jesus and Good Friday," she answered.

"How can that be?" I said, puzzled.

"Well, our Savior was crucified on Good Friday. And wasn't that the most awful day in history?"

"Sure," I said, still wondering what she was leading up to.

"What happened three days later?"

Suddenly, the light went on. Of course, Easter and Jesus' glorious Resurrection.

Noting the understanding in my eyes, she tousled my hair. "When troubles come, Michael, wait three days. Somehow, in some way, you'll see that everything begins to work out all right."

Again it had been proven. In fact, the new building turned out to be even better than we had originally thought. As operations were beginning, Michael came up to me in excitement.

"Dad, did you realize that this building has a room with thick concrete walls, ideal for our ovens and cleaning equipment? I can't believe it. It looks as if this place were made for us."

"I believe it was, Michael," I had to admit. "I believe it was."

For some time afterward I found myself thinking of the lesson of the fire.

From an earthly standpoint it seemed a tragedy, with our factory, cores, finished products, and company records all lost. For a time, while thinking only of the material, I had been tempted to give up. Not until we looked up, placed our hands in His, and stepped ahead in faith, did we come out in better shape than before the fire.

An extra blessing in all this was another lesson learned in finding God's guidance, or, as I like to say, "walking in the Spirit." Walking in the Spirit is being receptive to God's will in our lives, being open to His "nudges," seeing His guidance in everyday circumstances. Walking in the Spirit is listening to God's inspiration instead of giving in to one's mortal negativism. As we are told in Psalms 16:7 (TLB), "I will bless the Lord who counsels me; he gives me wisdom in the night. He tells me what to do."

It was something, I believe, we all found easier to do after the fire. Michael, for example, told me that instead of giving in to a natural despair after suffering the first shock of the fire, he asked himself the important question: *What does God want me to do next?*

"Somehow, in some way, He would always show me," said Michael. "When I got that terrible call at six o'clock in the morning, I had no one to turn to. You were in Florida. So, as I drove down to our plant, I kept praying for His direction.

"And you know, Dad, it came. What would have been a nightmare for me turned out all right. I was able to give the police and fire marshall all the information they needed. And it was no problem getting hold of our insurance adjuster.

"I'll always remember walking through the still smoking rubble that icy day with our adjuster. He'd reach down, pick up a charred piece of power-steering pump, and ask, 'How much is this part worth? What does it do? Where did you buy it? How many did you have on hand?'

"Somehow I was able to give him the right answers, something which I'm sure I could never have done on my own."

More and more we found ourselves going to the Lord for answers. And though each of us prayed for guidance individually, something happened one morning that turned out to be a prophecy for the future.

I was at my desk thinking about a new product for our line and was just starting to pray about it when my son walked in with Sam Lepore, a man who had been with us a few years.

It seemed to be a divine intervention. "Fellows," I said, "would you join me in prayer? I've been wondering whether or not we should take on remanufacturing distributors and was just going to the Lord about it."

"Sure, Dad," said Michael. Sam nodded thoughtfully, and the two of them sat down with me. Together we prayed for His guidance. Soon several of our men, including all of our foremen, were gathering together in my office at the start of the day for direction and inspiration. Each morning one of us would read a passage from the Bible. Often we shared personal concerns.

Something happened in those meetings. I felt a closer relationship among us, a greater sense of communication. Men who came bowed down with concerns usually left with heads lifted high.

One morning I discerned trouble as the men gathered around. It was easy to see; two of the foremen had been in conflict and the air was thick with animosity. Earlier in the week they had almost come to blows after some name calling. I read aloud from Matthew 5:21, 22 in The Living Bible: "Under the laws of Moses the rule was, 'If you murder, you must die.' But I have added to that rule, and tell you that if you are only *angry*, even in your own home, you are in danger of judgment! If you call your friend an idiot, you are in danger of being brought before the court. And if you curse him, you are in danger of the fires of hell."

The room was quiet for a long time. I looked up to see both foremen staring at the floor. Then they glanced at each other sheepishly and when they left the office they were walking together.

One morning one of our suppliers happened to come by while our prayer meeting was in progress. Afterward when he came into my office he was shaking his head. "Mike, I believe in prayer all right, but I don't see how you can mix it with business."

I told him about Emil Fava, one of the first men who joined our group. Emil wasn't a trained engineer but he had a spiritual discernment on mechanical things. One morning a supervisor brought up a problem on one of the assembly lines that had been defying solution. Several men had worked on it to no avail.

We prayed about it and after the meeting Emil came up to me. "Mr. Cardone, lock me away with that problem; I'll try to figure it out."

And that's exactly what we did. We gave him a little room and a desk and didn't bother him. Day after day he'd sit in there, studying pieces of equipment, popping out to the assembly line every once in a while to try something new. He hardly said a word to any of us but one could tell his mind was racing every minute.

After two weeks he proudly came into my office. "You see, Mr. Cardone, if we would just make this adjustment, and add another sequence to the line, we'd. . . ."

It worked!

Though not a university graduate, Emil had a real gift. He became our first quality control engineer. I was learning that when we discern an employee's gift and put him or her in a job where it could blossom or grow, the employee and company both benefit. Emil Fava died in 1983. Our new Quality Control Lab was dedicated in his memory a year later.

When we interview applicants, we pray for God's will concerning them. And often we hire people with no real idea of what work they'll do. Our first objective is to find out if God wants them with our company or not.

Resumes are not all that important, I've learned. All they tell you is what the individual has been doing. But I found that by really talking with a person, exploring his hopes, his aims, and what he enjoys doing, one can get an idea of his real gifts.

To that end we've learned to rotate a new employee among various jobs in the plant. For example, we may start an accountant in the core room, cleaning heavy dirty cores, and then move him to the packing department before giving him his final assignment. In this way the new employee gains a comprehensive view of how his job fits into the overall picture. Sometimes he finds he's happiest in an entirely new kind of job with us instead of the one for which he had applied. As we're told in Romans 12:6 (TLB), "God has given each of us the ability to do certain things well."

When a person is happy in his work, he or she is most productive. That's why we ask new applicants, "Are you willing to work where you are best fitted?"

A case in point was James Squiccimara, my uncle, who we all called Uncle Jimmy Mark. When he came on board in 1974 he smoked one stogie after another, cursed a blue streak, and was one of the brashest men I knew. Michael blanched when I decided to hire him.

"Dad, I can't understand it," he said. "You want a guy like that around *here?*"

"I know," I admitted, "but there's something about him I like."

"Well," said Michael dubiously, "go ahead, but I still don't know what you see in him."

Uncle Jimmy Mark became our plant superintendent and his special gift soon came to the fore. Underneath his rough exterior was not only a deep compassion for his fellow man but an appetite for hard work. He was brash, yes. When he'd see a man huffing and puffing trying to move a crate, he'd nudge him away and do it himself. It was his way of saying, "Let me help you, brother." Though tenderhearted, he shrank from letting anyone see it.

The toughest, grimiest task was his challenge. Often I would find a terrible mess being cleaned up by a man so covered with dirt and grease he was unrecognizable. When he'd turn around, all I could see were white eyeballs and shining teeth exposed in a big smile. It was usually Jimmy Mark. He is now with the Lord; our Plant Number 14 was dedicated in his honor by Oral Roberts.

And then there was Tony Lombardi. He was a barber by trade, but I thought he'd make an excellent core buyer. To look at Tony, a meticulous dresser who always had a manicure, you'd think him the last person to be sent out to buy cores. Core buyers go out through the country dealing with junkyards and core brokers. There are no published price sheets and the buying is a wheeling and dealing kind of thing.

My son, who knew Tony as both a barber and close family friend, again thought I was making a mistake.

"That's because when you were a little boy he used to twist the ears of the kids who were naughty in church," I laughed, "and I know you received your share."

Tony turned out to be one of the best core buyers in the business. Not only did he have a shrewd eye in getting cores at the best prices, but he was discerning about what we bought. Often he'd pass up what I felt was a good deal.

"Mike," he'd say when I'd questioned him, "that batch of power-steering pumps has been battered around too much; they just aren't the quality we look for in rebuilding."

He also kept a sharp eye on our inventories. If he felt we were reaching an overstock situation on one item, he'd be right in my office. "Mike, let's lay off wiper motors for a while," or, "We've enough steering pumps in stock now so we don't have to buy any more until I can make the best deal."

Tony was also a good barber. In fact, he kept his shop going by hiring other barbers to staff it. But God knew, I believe, that Tony was happiest when he was out hunting the raw materials that kept our company going.

Again, it's not always having the right college training or background expertise that makes a man or woman the best choice for a particular job. It's the spirit of the individual that counts. And if we, with the help of God, can discern this, we can't ask for anything more.

The best illustration of this I've seen was the following "employee evaluation," which I understand appeared in a management newsletter. I wish I knew who wrote it because it says it so very well.

STAFF TEAM EVALUATION

TO: Jesus, Son of Joseph
        Woodcrafters Carpenter Shop
        Nazareth 25922

FROM: Jordan Management
         Consultants
         Jerusalem 26544

Dear Sir:

Thank you for submitting the resumes of the twelve men you have picked for management positions in your new organization. All of them have now taken our battery of tests; and we have not only run the results through our computer, but also arranged personal interviews for each of them with our psychological and vocational aptitude consultant.

The profiles of all tests are included, and you will want to study each of them carefully. As part of our service and for your guidance, we make some general comments, much as an auditor will include some general statements. This is given as a result of staff consultation and comes without any additional fee.

It is the staff opinion that most of your nominees are lacking in background, education and vocational aptitude for the type of enterprise you are undertaking. They do not have the team concept. We would recommend that you continue your search for persons of experience in managerial ability and proven capacity.

Simon Peter is emotionally unstable and given to fits of temper. Andrew has absolutely no qualities of leadership. The two brothers, James and John, the sons of Zebedee, place personal interest above company loyalty. Thomas demonstrates a questioning attitude that would tend to undermine morale.

We feel that it is our duty to tell you that Matthew has been blacklisted by the Greater Jerusalem Better Business Bureau. James, the son of Alphaeus, and Thaddaeus definitely have radical leanings, and they both registered a high score on the manic-depressive scale.

One of the candidates, however, shows great potential. He is a man of ability and resourcefulness, meets people well, has a keen business mind and has contacts in high places. He is highly motivated, ambitious and responsible. We recommend Judas Iscariot as your controller and right-hand man. All of the other profiles are self-explanatory.

We wish you every success in your new venture.

Sincerely yours,
Jordan Management Consultants

Of course, I cannot believe Jesus made a mistake in choosing the man the management consultants felt best suited for the job. God had His own purpose in mind.

But we certainly made a mistake when we hired a man I'll call Jack Adams. I don't believe we were really discerning when we hired him. He seemingly had so much to offer that I let the world pull the wool over my eyes. Jack Adams, whose integrity seemed beyond question, was so bright and willing that I felt he was exactly what we needed. But he almost destroyed our company.

"Points to Remember"

(1) Through faith and prayer, desperation can become determination. Remember, "all things work together for good to them that love God . . ." (Romans 8:28).

(2) ". . . Man looketh on the outward appearance, but the Lord looketh on the heart" (1 Samuel 16:7).

Nine

Building a Body

I couldn't believe what Michael was telling me.

"You mean Jack Adams resigned?" I asked.

Michael looked down at the floor. "Yes," he said sadly, "we can't understand it. We offered him more money, responsibility, anything to keep him."

"But he left, just like that?"

Michael nodded. "There was nothing we could do."

Afterward, I sat at my desk thinking about Jack Adams. He had joined us about two years ago, a middle-aged man with no experience in remanufacturing operations. But there was something special about the man, an ingenuity and perceptive mind that I felt would eventually be a real contribution to our company.

That was in 1974, not long after we had moved from our Clearfield location to a new plant at 4435 North Philip Street. Our business was expanding and we had added distributors to our line. (The distributor controls the firing of a car engine's pistons.) Again, it was a product that other firms had ignored, and again, we found there was a demand for it by thrifty motorists. We now had 135 employees with a plant covering over an acre in floor space. Production was booming. Our new plant was a far cry from the little store we had started only four years earlier.

Jack Adams had promised to be the supervisor who would help us continue to grow. We had hired him eagerly.

Now as I sat drumming the desk with my fingers, I wondered about the man. Something undefinable seemed to be missing from him when he came on board. But in our eagerness to hire him, we had not prayed him in as much as with our other applicants.

However, Jack was personable, open-minded, and eager to learn. He willingly started from the bottom, eventually handling every remanufacturing job. When the dirty and grimy cores would come in, he and others would disassemble the units and carefully inspect and test each part. If an item, such as a valve or piston, were imperfect or incapable of restoration, it would be junked. Then the basic parts, such as pump castings, would be put through a Wheelabrator machine to remove corrosion and rust down to the bare pristine metal. Phosphate baths would protect the metal from future corrosion.

The parts would then go onto the assembly line where the pump would be reassembled using restored or brand-new parts. After testing and retesting, sometimes as much as five times, each employee who worked on the product would affix his or her personal mark of identification with the same pride as a silversmith who stamps a finished creation.

I remembered pointing out to Jack on the power-steering pumps that, unlike other remanufacturers, we include the pulley and reservoir cans with the pumps, making it easier and simpler for the mechanic to install.

"It costs us more," I said, "but it brings us a greater return in customer satisfaction and more return orders.

"You know, as the Lord told us," I continued, "a good workman should give more than his share."

I waited for Jack's reaction but it was little. Jack claimed to be a Christian, but the more time we spent together, the more I sensed that he was a weak, immature Christian.

"Oh well," I told Frances one night, "I think Jack will grow the longer he stays with us."

Frances, who was doing some sewing, bit off a thread, but said nothing. I suppose I should have been suspicious when Jack wondered why we tested each A-1 product before it was packaged.

"Why not test every fifth one like they do in a lot of plants?" he suggested. "That way the line would move a lot faster."

Remembering my testing of the vacuum wiper motors I rebuilt in Bonney's garage many years ago, I said, "This way, Jack, we can make a long-time, and in some cases a lifetime, warranty.

"I suppose," I smiled, "it could be called the lazy man's way of doing business."

"Lazy?" he asked.

"Sure," I said, "this way you avoid all the trouble and hassle in trying to placate an angry customer.

"Besides," I added, "it lets me sleep at night. I'd lay awake knowing that some family's life depended on an untested power-steering unit that we had supplied."

Eventually I put Jack second in command on the plant floor. He also did some of our purchasing and had access to our vendors and distributors. To learn he had left us crushed me. We had put so much time into his training, so much hope in his future. His leaving left a big hole and all of us had to do a lot of scurrying around to fill it. But that wasn't the worst of it.

About a month later Michael came in and slumped down next to my desk.

"Ready for this one, Dad?" he sighed.

"For what?"

"We just learned that Jack Adams and someone else have gone into competition with us in a rebuilding business only a few miles away."

I stared at Michael. "Don't tell me," I ventured, "don't tell me he's remanufacturing the same products?"

Michael stared at the floor and nodded. "And it seems that the other fellow who's put up the money doesn't have any scruples. We've discovered that the two of them are going after our customers by undercutting our prices."

I sighed and looked out the window. So what else was new in this world of ours? But that wasn't all. We later found out that he was trying to lure some of our best employees by offering them a nickel or dime more per hour.

"He's promising them the moon," said Michael.

And some believed him, for several of our people gave their resignations. Now we were really being hurt. Losing people was like parting with members of my family. For by then our company had become a family.

Anger filled me. How could someone do that and profess to be a Christian? Then I remembered the words of a wise theologian who said, "Because some people are inoculated with small doses of Christianity, they don't catch the real thing."

Going after our customers and employees wasn't the end of it, however. For some years we had worked with an outside engineer, whom I'll call Smith. With our direction and financial help, Smith had developed a unique automated machine used in our remanufacturing. It gave us a competitive edge in the market, or so we thought. One day one of our vice-presidents came into the office shaking his head.

"I happened to drive by Jack Adams's place today and what do you think I saw? There was Smith unloading a duplicate of the machine he had made for us!"

"That dog in the manger!" I flushed and then simmered down. After all, didn't the Lord say that vengeance was His? I relaxed and put Adams, Smith, and everything else bothering me about the situation into God's hands and left it there. I had a business to run. What happened to Adams and the way he was handling things was up to the Lord.

And a business to run we had. We had already outgrown our premises on Philip Street which had been doubled in size. After much prayer and searching, we had found additional space of some 38,000 square feet in a building at 4327-37 North American Street. We had grown to 170 employees and were fast developing a reputation as the country's largest supplier of remanufactured wiper motors, distributors, and power-steering pumps.

Jack Adams? His company chewed him up and spit him out after getting all they could out of him. The firm itself did not maintain product quality, made mistakes, became known for unreliability, and within five years went out of business.

If Jack Adams had left a bad taste in my mouth, I only had to think of men like Mark Spuler, John Tedesco, Joe Beretta, Allan Giordano, and other loyal employees.

These men had really been prayed into our company and perhaps, like the men analyzed in that engineering management newsletter, in the world's eye they were not exactly suited for the work to which they had been called. More and more I was seeing the truth in Psalms 16:3, "I want the company of the godly man and woman in the land; they are the true nobility."

Mark Spuler, who became our Executive Vice-President, was a sociology major and Allan Giordano, our Senior Vice-President of Marketing, was a potato chip salesperson before coming to us. I learned from them as much as they learned from me.

Mark taught me to swallow my pride. He joined us in June 1972 after graduating with honors from Oral Roberts University. He gave up a valuable scholarship to Oklahoma State University to become a disassembler of power-steering pumps at three dollars an hour. Whenever I'd see him, blackened with grease, working on pump cores, he'd look up and smile. Even then I felt he had a real future with us.

But Mark felt led to the mission field and he and his wife left us for evangelical work in Spain. Frankly, I felt hurt, even though I knew he was obviously following the Lord's guidance. After completing their six months' mission work, Mark and his wife returned to Philadelphia. He didn't ask for his job back because I'm sure he knew how I felt about his leaving. And, with pride in my way, I did not ask him to return.

But pride is a sin and one afternoon at a get-together who should be there but Mark and his wife. I swallowed my pride and asked him to come back. I don't know who was happiest about it, Mark or I.

John Tedesco, Senior Vice-President of Sales, joined us a year later, followed by Allan Giordano, Senior Vice-President of Marketing, two years later, and Joe Beretta, Vice-President of Engineering, who joined us in 1976. The other M. Cardone Industries vice-presidents, listed in order of the year they joined us, are the following: Evan Curry, Vice-President Quality Control, 1977; Peter Calo, Executive Vice-President, 1978; Dom Foti, Vice-President Remanufacturing, 1978; Paul Spuler, Vice-President Administration, 1978; Daniel George, Vice-President American Street Division, 1979; Dave Genca, Vice-President Data Processing, 1981; John Pacitti, Vice-President Financial Operations, 1982; Dave Hernandez, Vice-President Master Cylinder Remanufacturing, 1982; Sam Hernandez, Vice-President Distribution, 1982; and Frank Zgrablich, Vice-President Human Resources, 1985.

All these men have contributed much to our company, and most of them, when hired, were not highly technical people. Maybe that was a point in our favor.

In 1974 we felt a strong leading to investigate the remanufacturing of master cylinders. This unit is the vital center of an automobile's braking system. The car's brake pedal moves a piston inside the master cylinder that forces hydraulic fluid through the system to actuate the brake shoes' grip on each wheel. If the master cylinder fails, accidents can happen.

In checking around we found a few firms selling rebuilt master cylinders. In truth this was a misnomer for in many cases they were taking used master cylinders from junked or wrecked cars. Without taking them apart to inspect each piece, they tested them to see if they worked, then cleaned off the dirt and grease and repainted them. They looked "new" and, at the time of purchase, worked. But how long would it be before one gave out? Three months? Six months? A driver wouldn't know until it might be too late. As Proverbs 16:11 (TLB) taught, "The Lord demands fairness in every business deal. He established this principle," and to us this meant quality workmanship.

We never had worked, nor would work, that way. To carry the A-1 label we believed that a master cylinder had to be completely taken apart with each element carefully inspected. If anything were worn in any way, it had to be replaced by a brand-new part so that the finished master cylinder met our specifications of "as good as new or better."

Daily, I am driven to squeeze more and more quality into our products. I've told my managers a thousand times: The only job security anybody has in this company comes from quality—the only ingredient for satisfied customers.

Experts in the field said it couldn't be done. They claimed it was economically impossible to remanufacture a master cylinder to precision standards and still be able to sell it for less than the cost of a brand-new one. Yet deep in my heart, I felt it could be done. In our little prayer sessions around my desk we asked the Lord for guidance. And in keeping our minds open to the Lord we also kept our ears open to our employees and anyone else that could help us.

By now open forum discussions were the rule with us. If someone had an idea, as crazy as it might seem, we encouraged them to bring it up. No one would be ridiculed and each idea was gratefully accepted. I remembered the story about the General Electric light bulb. For years men in the firm's laboratory played a standing joke on new employees by assigning them to find a way of frosting light bulbs on the inside. It was a joke because everyone knew it was impossible technically. But along came a young apprentice who, in testing some crazy ideas, found a way to do it. As a result, no one in our discussion groups felt self-conscious about expressing what they thought.

We also listened to our machine suppliers plus manufacturers of brand-new master cylinders with whom we had established good relationships. Many OEMs (original equipment manufacturers) had learned new techniques from us, as we had learned from them. As the Bible says, ". . . in multitude of counsellors there is safety" (Proverbs 24:6).

I'll never forget the day Michael, Mark, Joe, and the others proudly showed me our new master-cylinder remanufacturing line. It was complex, to say the least, but it worked. Some of the parts that we automatically replaced were the rubber elements such as the vital piston cups. Even though rubber might look perfect, it can deteriorate and these parts could eventually fail. We couldn't take that chance and so manufactured new rubber seals to high specifications from our own molds.

Our main problem was the pitting inside the master cylinder. This is probably why industry experts said that practical remanufacturing couldn't be done. The pitting comes from corrosion inside the cylinder. This results in a roughened uneven cylinder wall and thus a poor seal for the piston plunging through it. Brake fluid seeps past the piston and the pedal becomes mushy, sometimes useless. The only way to correct this was to hone the cylinder wall to a mirror finish.

For the first year or two our people manually operated the honing machine, carefully computing to a thousandth of an inch how much material in each case had to be removed. One day Michael came in to my office with some frightening facts and figures.

"It doesn't look like we're going to make it with master cylinders," he said. "They're costing us too much to remanufacture to be able to sell them less than the price of new ones."

"What's the main problem?" I asked.

"Honing the cylinder walls," replied Michael. "The operator can't punch these out like buttons. The honing of each cylinder must be done on an individual basis depending on the condition of the wall. And when you're talking about differences of a few thousandths of an inch, it takes time for precision adjusting.

"What can we do?" I wondered.

"I don't know," said Michael. "We'll just have to have some brainstorming on this."

Again our people got together in a brainstorming session. It was an all-for-one and one-for-all spirit; as in the past, no one worried about who got the credit for ideas. If it worked, our company would benefit and thus all would benefit. More and more we were becoming like the body of Christ, described as follows: "And whether one member suffer, all the members suffer with it; or one member be honoured, all the members rejoice with it" (1 Corinthians 12:26).

Again, we sought the Lord's guidance and He was true to His Word, "Seek and ye shall find." For in working with our suppliers, we were able to come up with a high-speed honing machine that automatically compensated for varying tolerances. Instead of honing hundreds a day, we were able to process thousands and thus keep our prices down.

When industry experts said it couldn't be done, our team would go ahead and do it. It reminded me of the lesson of the bumblebee. Because of its small wing area and large body, scientists say that according to the laws of aerodynamics, it cannot fly. But the bumblebee doesn't know this and goes ahead and flies anyway.

Master cylinders became one of our largest lines. Interestingly, when we began remanufacturing them in 1974, they were an insignificant part of the rebuilt business, probably accounting for about 10 percent of overall replacements. Today, some 70 percent of replacements are remanufactured.

However, success in this field led us into trouble. In 1986

some major manufacturers of new master cylinders set out to reverse the above figures by cutting their prices close to ours. In addition one major manufacturer launched a major advertising blitz on television and in magazines in an endeavor to win our customers.

M. Cardone Industries, Inc.,* was in a spot. We shared our concern with employees asking, "How can we get our manufacturing costs down and still maintain quality?"

To picture our plight, we thumbtacked big advertisements of the new equipment firms pushing their new master cylinders on our factory bulletin boards. The message was simple. I couldn't help but chuckle, when walking through the plant one day, I overheard two assembly line workers talking about the problem.

"Do you think we'll get any awards for meeting our competition?" asked one.

"Yeah," grinned the other. "We'll get to keep our jobs."

Ideas and suggestions began pouring in.

"We're handling some parts twice," one employee pointed out. "Here's a way of combining these two operations and doing a better job."

Others came up with cost-saving and waste reduction innovations on the use of chemicals and other materials. Some suggestions were as simple as a way of getting an extra day's wear out of a pair of work gloves. All of them contributed. And with everyone working harder and smarter, we were able to offer our usual high-quality product at even lower prices to retain our share of the market.

Again and again M. Cardone Industries employees rose to the occasion when an emergency developed. In 1976 a terrible fire roared through our automated paint-spraying opera-

*By now M. Cardone Industries, Inc., had become our official corporate identification.

tion. It was bad enough but when the insurance people were installing a new fire-control system, they accidentally started another conflagration. As a result our automated paint-spraying operation in which A-1 products received their unique blue coating was shut down for twelve days. Into the gap jumped employees who hand-sprayed units as they came off the assembly lines so we could maintain our vital inventory.

Again and again I was amazed at the way in which M.C.I. people faced formidable challenges.

In 1984 when a new roof was being installed on Plant Number 12, a heavy nighttime rainstorm broke through temporary covers and flooded the plant with six inches of water. By eleven o'clock the next morning with everyone working together the plant was cleaned up and put back in production.

Two years later Plant Number 14 was shut down completely one winter's day when a forklift truck accidentally ruptured a heater gas line sending fumes dangerously close to the other heaters. Employees were quickly evacuated and dock doors thrown open to help dissipate the gas. With repairs quickly completed everyone was back to work within an hour.

None of these challenges could have been met without our people throwing themselves wholeheartedly into the breach to remedy the problem as soon as possible.

What is responsible for this enthusiasm and teamwork? One could say it's because we provide employees a safe, comfortable working environment with a wide variety of benefits from medical to retirement, plus opportunities for advancement. But I believe it is something more than this, something unseen and yet so powerful to be almost unbelievable.

"Points to Remember"

(1) It is important to "pray in" prospective employees to know the Lord's will for your company.

(2) When the employees become like a family, each equipped with a concern for one another, problems don't loom as large.

Ten

A Wind
of the Spirit

I t all happened so unexpectedly. But then, who can antici-
pate the moving of God?

By the end of 1978 M. Cardone Industries was continuing
its expansion with eight plants in operation covering almost
150,000 square feet of floor space and almost 400 employees.
By this time we were remanufacturing eight different auto
parts including wiper motors, power-steering pumps, distributors, master cylinders, power-steering pumps, control
valves, and gear boxes. Soon we went into power-brake
boosters and blower motors, which we followed by rack-and-
pinion steering units.

And yet, as we continued expanding, something impressed me that adding new lines wasn't the *real reason* God had in mind for our growth. In quiet moments my mind would drift back to when I first found the Lord: *Did God want me to become a minister?*

I remembered when in asking my old mentor, Brother Antonio, about it, how he would smile and say: "Mike, just keep asking God for direction; He knows what you should do. And if you keep close to Him, He will guide you. It may be His will for you to become a preacher, a missionary, or. . ." He paused thoughtfully for a moment, and added: "Or, He may want you to become a good businessman, a Christian businessman.

"God knows," he added quietly, "our world needs more of them."

Well, I had become a businessman, and I had tried to be a Christian. Yet it seemed God was asking for something more. His will became clearer to me during an early morning prayer meeting in my office in January 1979. By now these 6:45 A.M. get-togethers were attended by most of our supervisors who said they found them to be the most important part of their day.

Something special happened in this January meeting. As Stan Karol, an employee who also served as a minister after working hours, led us in prayer, the Spirit of God seemed to sweep over us. We found ourselves on our knees singing, praying in tongues, arms on each others' shoulders, in a real spirit of togetherness. Wouldn't it be wonderful, I thought, if *all* our employees could share this same joy?

It was then I began to see the real reason God wanted me to start this business back in 1970. He wanted to be invited to work in *every* phase of it, in every square inch of the plants, in every assembly line process, in the life of every employee. He would be our senior partner.

When our prayer session had ended, I expressed my vision to the men in the room.

"Do you think something like this can work here, in an industrial plant?" I asked.

The room was silent for a moment. Then my son spoke quietly, "Remember Penny Smith?"

In 1974 Penny had a supervisory post in Plant Number 1. We only had about 135 employees at the time. I had an odd feeling about her shortly after she was hired. It was the way she tossed her head when I saw our Plant Manager at the time, talking to her. When I'd say "hello" in passing by her work station, she would mutter a guarded reply. So I wasn't too surprised when Mark Spuler, our Executive Vice-President, called me one afternoon to say she had been causing trouble in the factory.

"For the last two weeks she's been fighting me tooth and nail on every problem that comes up, Mr. Cardone. It seems I'm spending all my time arguing with her."

"What seems to be her complaint?"

"Everything," he replied. "No matter what we do—move an employee to a new work station, give someone overtime, or dock someone for repeatedly coming in late—she's right there making a mountain out of a molehill."

"Well, Mark," I said, "you know what you have to do if worse comes to worse."

"Sure, Mr. Cardone," he replied, "it'll be a relief to get her out of our hair."

An hour later Mark was back on the phone, his voice tense. "Mr. Cardone, I brought Penny into the office and told her that if she was unhappy working here, she could leave."

"Did she?" I asked.

"No, she blew up. She screamed that she wasn't leaving, that in fact she'll have the doors of our plant blocked up so tight that not even you or I could get to work."

"Where is she now?" I asked.

"She's in my office; I had told her she was being fired for insubordination and when she became a raging maniac, I slipped out to another phone to call you."

"Well, try and calm her, Mark. Keep me posted; the rest of us here will pray for you and Penny."

"Thanks, Mr. Cardone, prayer is the only thing that can help right now."

When I told my son, he said, "Should we go down there and help Mark?"

"No," I answered, "I think he can handle it. The best thing we can do is pray for him."

Ten minutes passed . . . twenty . . . thirty . . . an hour. I was getting tense. My son kept glancing at me. I even caught myself wondering if we should continue to stay out of it.

At five o'clock in the afternoon the phone rang and I grabbed it. It was Mark.

"Mr. Cardone," he explained, "it was rough going. Penny ran out into the plant screaming that she was going to kill herself. She dug a vial of pills out of her purse and shook them at me."

Sweat beaded on my forehead. "What did you do?"

"One of the other men in the plant helped me take her back into my office, where she slumped down and began crying heavily. I sat with her and let her cry herself out. When she finally stopped, I took her hand, told her that someone far bigger than any one of us loved her deeply and wanted the best for her."

I silently breathed thanks.

"She really wanted to know who it was, Mr. Cardone," continued Mark. "And when I told her about Jesus and the salvation He offered, she prayed the sinner's confession with me and gave her heart to the Lord."

"Bless you, Mark," I sighed.

"For the next hour and a half we read the Bible together to where she began to understand some of its teaching and principles."

Mark's voice sounded thrilled. "Mr. Cardone, I think we have a new person in Penny; she's not only coming to work tomorrow but wants to join a church."

"Hallelujah!" I shouted.

Penny Smith not only joined a church but began living every day of her life for Christ. In getting to know her better, we learned what had driven her to such irrational behavior. Her husband was an abusive alcoholic who gave her no help in dealing with an errant son.

We supported her in prayer and friendship. And though, sadly, her husband died of his ailment, Penny was able to help her son find real meaning in life. She continued with us and was one of our finest employees for a good number of years.

I leaned back thinking about the peace and tranquility Penny Smith possessed after she found God. And when, some years later, she learned she was suffering from cancer, she was able to continue on in the same joy and self-confidence.

I knew what Michael meant when he asked if I remembered Penny Smith. God was already involved in every phase of our business. He was there with Mark Spuler and Penny. He was here with us today.

But how could we give every employee an opportunity to relate to Him every day and not on a hit-or-miss basis as with Penny who found Him when it was almost too late? I brought this up to the men around me. Ideas began percolating, and I sensed a rising enthusiasm in the room.

"All our people should have the opportunity to meet together."

"But how? We don't have enough space for everyone to assemble in one place."

"Why not have each department meet individually? The supervisor could be the leader."

"Hey, that's a great idea. And think of the opportunity for communication. If someone has a complaint or problem, he or she can easily bring it up in the meeting."

"But what if someone objects to taking part in the prayer? Not all of our people are Christians, you know."

"Well, we can have the Scripture reading and prayer at the close. If someone doesn't wish to participate in this, he or she doesn't have to."

"But when should we have these get-togethers? Weekly?"

"No, every day."

"Before work begins?"

"During regular business hours. We want to pay them for their time."

"But when?"

I leaned back in my chair remembering something a jeweler friend had told me back in Pittston. In the days of spring-wound pocket watches, the kind the engineers and trainmen used on the railroads, I had an old one that needed repair. I brought it to a watchmaker who was a friend of the family and, handing it back to me after it was fixed, he said that it was a good idea to wind my watch in the morning.

"Nothing like starting the day on a strong spring," he said.

Of course, I thought. And nothing like starting the day on a strong prayer. We made our announcement.

Since plant operations begin at 7:30 A.M., we stated that each department would meet together as a team at that time for a five-minute session before work started. During this period the meeting would be open for all comments, whether it was a suggestion for improving a work process, a complaint, or a personal concern that needed sharing. Then the department leader would close with a passage of Scripture and prayer. If anyone wished to skip the latter because of different beliefs, they were welcome to do so.

Then we held our breaths. How would people react? After the first week the answer was clear. The supervisors were enthusiastic.

"The ideas that come out of those five minutes are terrific," said one. "One of the girls suggested a better way of assembling a valve, another felt a new fluorescent light over her area would help her work better. Best of all," he went on, "there's a new spirit of camaraderie in our group, a more friendly, open feeling."

And practically no one objected to the Scripture reading and prayer.

"Everybody in my group appreciated asking God for a good day and safety on the job," reported one supervisor.

Years later when Michael, Jr., went to Japan to study its industries' manufacturing methods, which have been so successful in terms of high employee morale, efficiency, and quality production, he found departmental team meetings in operation similar to ours.

However, the success of our team meetings generated a new problem. As one of our supervisors put it at a devotional in my office, "It's wonderful the way my people are asking for prayer and advice on personal concerns, but now it's happening all through the day."

Another added, "Yeah, I love counseling with folks but lately I've had trouble finding the time to even eat my lunch."

Good news, and not so good news. On one hand the problem proved that our team meetings were filling a real need. On the other hand I could certainly sympathize with the supervisor who was busy enough as it was with his own work.

I knew, however, that God hadn't given us this idea of team meetings without giving us an answer for our dilemma. And so at our devotional meeting in my office we all asked God to show us what to do.

There was silence for a moment after we finished. Then someone said, "You know, what we really need is someone on hand who is trained to handle the employees' personal problems, who can give full time to the people."

"Like a chaplain?" another asked.

"Sure."

My heart quickened.

Paul Spuler, vice-president in charge of administration who had joined us in 1978, mentioned something in an off-hand way that seemed to bring it all together. "I just happened to remember. My father-in-law, John Pagano, is leaving his pastorate in Malaga, New Jersey, where he has been for fifteen years."

I knew the man! "Oh my," I exclaimed, "if there were ever the kind of pastor we need, it's someone like Brother Pagano!"

Within two weeks John Pagano, an Assembly of God minister, had come on board as our chaplain. With a congregation of some fifteen hundred people, considering he also ministered to our employees' families, he probably became the busiest pastor in Philadelphia.

Shortly after he joined us I had visible evidence of the difference a chaplain can make in the business world. Every employee was encouraged to bring any need or problem to

Chaplain Pagano in his office. However, he knew that some people would be too bashful or embarrassed to do this. So he took it on himself to circulate through the plants keeping his eyes open for any needs.

I soon learned how effective this was in one of our regular talks when he told me what happened one afternoon. While walking past the distributor assembly line, he noticed something about a young Puerto Rican woman that caught his attention. He walked over to her and, seeing a wedding band on her finger, greeted her.

"Hello, Señora, and how are you today?"

She looked down at her work and shrugged. But to Brother Pagano it was obvious that she had been crying.

"There is nothing so wrong that the Lord can't take care of it," he gently said.

She looked up, her dark eyes brimming with tears and shook her head, "Not my sorrow, Father, not my sorrow." Then she broke into heavy sobbing. Gently touching her shaking shoulders, he led her to a quiet corner where he let her cry herself out.

"Now daughter, how can I help?"

Between sobs she told him how she was having bitter marital problems. Brother Pagano prayed with her, assuring her that the Lord was already taking care of her situation. She wiped her eyes, thanked him effusively, and with a new lightness in her step went back to work. When the chaplain learned that her husband also worked with us, he went over to his work station some distance away and found the young man glumly packing wiper motors.

In their talk he admitted he had been unkind to his wife and was penitent. However, he felt she would not forgive him for some cruel things he had said. "And I deserve it, Pastor," he muttered.

Chaplain Pagano assured him that his wife had already forgiven him and by confessing his sin, God had forgiven him. The young man brightened and when the chaplain left him, he was packing wiper motors with new alacrity.

The next day the chaplain found two entirely new people, their faces shining. Later, both of their foremen told him that they had never seen such a change in workers. "Frankly," said one, "I was getting ready to recommend we let the fellow go. He wasn't working at all up to par, but now he's one of our best packers."

When I visited the two on the floor later and told them how happy I was to see their marriage restored, I wasn't expecting the gift I received in return.

"You know, Mr. Cardone," said the husband, who with his wife had immigrated from Puerto Rico, "this place has done something for me that I've found nowhere else in America. In the places I worked before, I felt like a burro. No one cared how I felt inside. All they were interested in was how many boxes I could move in a day.

"Here, I feel like a human being, like . . . ," his brown eyes brimming with tears, he continued haltingly, "I feel like someone really cares."

It was the best assurance I could have been given that our chaplaincy program was on its way to success.

There were many such emotional healings through the plant, thanks to our chaplain, and there were physical restorations, too. One day a woman walked into Brother Pagano's office complaining of a neck so stiff she could hardly move.

"I recommended she see a doctor," he said in telling me about it later, "but before she left the office we prayed together. I placed my hands on her neck asking God for His healing through the presence of His Son, Jesus Christ. Then she stood up and threw her arms into the air crying, 'I'm healed, I'm healed, I can move my stiff neck!' She walked out of my office praising God."

I, too, benefited from our chaplain. One morning as I struggled to find a solution for a problem in the plant, it suddenly dawned on me I wasn't taking advantage of all our resources. I left my office and about ten minutes later found Brother Pagano on one of his rounds. After explaining the problem, I asked him to pray for our need. By that evening, our problem was solved.

I wondered about this. Why does it often happen that the more people there are involved in praying for a need, the quicker it seems to be filled? I believe when one puts oneself in God's presence through prayer, one is receptive to His guidance. And the more people there are doing this concerning a problem, the greater opportunity for answers to come.

Thus through our morning team meetings and the work of our chaplain, prayers seemed to be answered more and more in our plant. Marriages were healed, work problems solved, and lives were changed. Counseling helped employees overcome financial difficulties, personal dilemmas, and family problems such as alcoholism and errant children.

Soon it became obvious one chaplain wasn't enough to meet the needs of our growing family and we hired Celso Hernandez, who was able to relate to our employees of Hispanic ancestry.

Of course, I took some ridicule from friends in the industry. "Put a chaplain on the payroll?" snorted one. "My firm's out to make a profit, not save souls. Besides, you can't mix business and religion!"

However, in studying the field, I realized we weren't the only company "mixing business and religion." I read that a few firms had pioneered the use of chaplains back in the 1950s.

In one article I read that Homer Good, the chaplain of a large trucking firm in the South, said, "People need someone to talk to about their innermost concerns. With us they can be absolutely frank without worry of our conversation going to management. And usually the problem stems from the same thing—the sufferer is dodging God or doesn't realize He can help.

"But," Good was quick to emphasize, "it takes sympathetic listening. And through the individual's own disclosure of himself and his problems, we try to help him understand what steps he must take to receive God's healing.

"For instance," he explained, "when one of our dock workers turned out to be an alcoholic, it would have been simple to fire him. But do you fire an employee who gets appendicitis? Alcoholism is a sickness, too. So we stayed with him and, through counseling, he learned why he drank—a deep-seated insecurity stemming from a rejection he suffered in childhood.

"We helped him find his security in God's love instead of the bottle. How is he today? His foreman recently told me he wished he had a hundred men like him."

The industrial chaplains I read about did not try to take the place of the employees' own pastors or rabbis.

"We're here just to supplement their work," one said.

"Yes, you get quite close to employees as a chaplain," another said thoughtfully. "And whether you're talking to a new man on the docks or a long-time executive, job categories don't count. It's just you, him, and God."

He brightened. "Being a chaplain can put you in a funny position, too. We had a strike some years back. And when I came to the terminal that morning, I met a picket line.

"'Who's side are *you* on, chaplain?' one man shouted.

"I thought for a second, then yelled back, '*The Lord's side!*'"

That chaplain's answer summed up the whole concept of the chaplain in industry—neither a tool of management nor representative of labor, but a symbol of God's wish for the best for both.

Through the years M. Cardone Industries has put six chaplains on staff, each serving one of the varied ethnic groups in our company. In June 1987 the twelve-year-old son of a Laotian couple who worked with us was accidentally shot by a playmate playing with a loaded pistol. Our Laotian chaplain, Howard Tanovan, stayed with the mother and father in the hospital, praying and encouraging them during the five hours of their son's surgery. As soon as we heard of it, we asked all our chaplains, employees, and various churches in the area to pray, for the boy was not expected to survive. For weeks he was in a coma and the day his mother was told he would probably be a vegetable, she put him in God's hands, praying all night for his healing.

The next day she visited her son, still comatose, touched his hand, and called his name: "Addie, Addie." Suddenly, the little fellow opened his eyes and started crying to his mother. Our whole plant was filled with excitement and as of this writing the boy is walking and attending school.

In addition to their counseling work our chaplains administrate a benevolence fund used to minister to employees' special needs when suffering extended illness and accidents. They also visit hospitalized employees and new mothers, all of whom are given fruit baskets. When employees are home ill, chaplains keep in daily contact with them through phone visits to ascertain their needs.

The success of our chaplaincy program generated another need. By early 1979, after our departmental team meetings had begun, the men praying in my office every morning were soon spilling out the door. In the meantime employees were seeking quiet places in which to pray. To fill this growing need, we built a chapel in Plant Number 1 at 4435 North Philip Street. This chapel, dedicated in March 1979 by Rex Humbard, became so popular that other chapels were opened in various plants, each one also dedicated by a leading figure in the ministry, including Carlton Pearson and Norman Vincent Peale.

In February 1980, when Dr. Peale dedicated our largest chapel in Plant Number Twelve at 5660 Rising Sun Avenue, he said, "I can pick up the Spirit of the Lord when I come into a place and it is here in this plant."

His observation heartened me for this had become our goal. Thus every morning before work starts, there are meetings in four different chapels open to all employees who wish to attend. Television monitors throughout the plant pipe in the chapel programs for those employees already present but unable to be in the chapel. During the noontime lunch hour Christian programs are broadcast through these video monitors.

Employee choirs, an outgrowth of these chapel meetings, sing at company functions and parties. Many reflect the various ethnic groups among our personnel as they sing in their own language.

As I hear these groups joyfully singing, I smile to myself, remembering the time some sixty years ago when I wondered if God wanted me to become a missionary to foreign shores. As it has worked out, people from many foreign shores have come to M. Cardone Industries, including Portuguese, Italians, Laotians, Cambodians, Puerto Ricans, Jamaicans, East Indians, Pakistanis, Hungarians, Vietnamese, Thai, Chinese, Romanians, Haitians, Peruvians, Colombians, and Afghans. Because we felt a responsibility for their spiritual growth, we endeavored to introduce them to various churches in the area.

However, these newcomers did not feel at home in typical American churches.

How could we help them? We were already offering in-plant Bible studies and monthly fellowship times with special speakers. But we knew it wasn't enough. Thus on January 13, 1984, we determined to provide as many of these groups as possible with churches of their own. We began by establishing them in our plant, ground familiar to them.

Of course, we had to find suitable chaplains for these churches to be called "New Life Centers." We prayed for direction and God began to open doors. A Portuguese pastor, Alvaro de Sousa, came to lead a fellowship on Sunday morning. A leader was found for our Spanish congregation that met Sunday afternoons. Two months later we found a pastor for our East Indian people and during the summer a former Buddhist priest, Sam Siam, dedicated to winning souls for Christ, came to work with our Southeast Asians.

Although we did not charge rent or gain monetarily from these New Life Centers, the letters I began receiving from employees were worth more than anything material. Luis Rodriguez wrote that he had been a lost and confused man on coming to America from Portugal. He had been lonely and worried about falling into a bad situation that would end up hurting him and his family. Then he came to our Portuguese New Life Center.

"The service was spoken in my own language and I began to sort out my confusion," he wrote. "Things started making sense to me during that service. What I heard and felt was enough to help me accept Jesus as my Savior and I started to understand why God not only led me to America but had inspired me to that chapel service. I really had found the new life I was looking for, a life with no traps and no evil, but full of blessings for me and my family."

Then there was Susete Rodriguez who, after attending our Portuguese New Life Center, wrote the following: "It was the first Portuguese Sunday service spoken in my own language. . . . At first I was not humble enough to recognize that I was a sinner needing salvation, and my mind was confused with dogmas and ideas. But the words I heard in that first service built in my mind a different picture of the reality concerning the things of God, causing me to replace those depreciating ideas with a consistent desire to follow the Gospel and submit my life to Jesus. That decision, with the better understanding of the Word of God through the Bible studies in the plant, and the good example of one of its chaplains, changed my life. I had a better attitude, and the blessings of God have always been present in me and my family. My prayers and reading God's Word keep me close with Him."

Bharat Jasani, who came from India, wrote that in his former religion he did not learn about a personal relationship with the Lord but gathered only with others as a group during festivals.

"At M. Cardone Industries' morning and weekly chapel services, I was touched by the hymns and the message of God which gave me insight into the Lord's plan for me. After attending weekly Bible studies, I accepted the Lord as my personal Savior which has changed the spiritual path of my life. Without it I would have been living in a dark unknown world."

As I read many letters like these, I had a vision of new churches being founded because of these young Christians. And that's exactly what happened. For the very success of these New Life Centers in our plants gave birth to churches in the community. Within a year after it began, the Spanish Center continued on its own as the Spanish "International Assembly of God."

A year after the Cambodian New Life Center began, it, too, reached the point where, with increasing membership it moved into its own facilities as the Cambodian Evangelical Church on Philadelphia's west side.

Supplementing the chapels, churches, and devotional meetings was our installation of a Family Fun Center, a large hall of about two thousand square feet, in Plant 13, at 5670 Rising Sun Avenue. It serves as an all-purpose room, filled with over seventy free-play arcade video games. M. Cardone Industries families can bring their children for fun nights, to play games, and later, if they wish, to listen to evangelistic speakers and Christian music.

The Family Center is also open for use by other churches in our area and most nights it is filled with laughter, music, and singing. One night as I walked by the center, some Indians were celebrating their Hindu New Year. I am glad that we at M. Cardone Industries have no restrictions against any non-Christian groups; our only criterion for joining our firm is a willingness to work and a desire to do one's best.

When one disgruntled employee, in an effort to cause trouble, complained to an outside agency of "compulsory" attendance at chapel meetings, one of our long-time employees, an atheist, stood up and said, "What d'ya mean? I've been working at M. Cardone Industries for ten years and never once attended one of those meetings. But, as far as I'm concerned, this is the best place I've ever worked in my life!"

Needless to say, the disgruntled employee's complaint was quickly dismissed.

One day after attending chapel services and noticing an employee huddled in consultation with one of our chaplains, I remembered back to when I was a youngster and wondered if God wanted me to become a minister.

I smiled when I thought of what happens when one gives oneself completely to God. He not only made me a businessman but helped me start a ministry with a parish of some twelve hundred people.

But it was still a company, a tough, lean enterprise dedicated to filling consumers' needs in the most efficient and economical way. However, M. Cardone Industries' marketing and distributing innovations could not have happened without God's guidance. And it came in some exciting ways.

"Points to Remember"

(1) You, like our chaplains, are an instrument in God's hand to touch the lives of others.
(2) Praying in agreement with others brings heaven's answer to our prayers.

Eleven

Nuts and Bolts of Success

Is God interested in the little everyday things of our lives, in the mundane affairs of, say, running a business?

Some acquaintances have pooh-poohed this thought, claiming, "God is too big to be bothered with such inconsequentials." On the contrary, I believe that our every thought, word, and deed are vitally important to Him. After all, doesn't the Bible tell us that a sparrow does not fall without His notice?

If I read my Bible right, God is vitally interested in our work. And if we endeavor to glorify Him in it, I know He will help us meet our responsibilities through His guidance. I believe it happens at M. Cardone Industries: We could not have made it past formidable roadblocks in marketing and distributing without His help.

Though the A-1 Remanufacturing brand name was well known in our local area, we faced a problem as we expanded into new marketing zones. I remember John Tedesco (now Senior Vice-President of Sales) returning dejected from sales trips back in the early 1970s.

"It was tough to convince the warehouse distributors who had never heard of us that our products were worth carrying," he recalls. "They found it difficult to believe that they could realize approximately thirty percent more profit selling our remanufactured parts over the sales of new ones." But John didn't let that stop him. He prayed about it and came up with an answer.

"I went out and sold orders to a dozen or so of the warehouse distributors' customers, who also were jobbers," he smiled. "Then I returned to the warehouse distributors and told them that if they didn't want to fill the orders, we'd ship them ourselves direct to the jobbers from our factory."

That's how A-1 remanufactured products became a staple on their shelves.

Slowly but surely we expanded our distribution across the country. But building a market took more than quality products and reasonable prices. A number of other rebuilders were out there selling similar products, some of them long before we came into the picture.

"What can you do for us that the other guy can't?" was the often-heard challenge. We knew we could offer unmatched product quality and dependability, but it was clear we had to come up with something more.

Our answer? New concepts in marketing that set us apart from the others. To develop them, we had to again put ourselves in our customers' shoes. As Jesus taught, ". . . whatso-ever ye would that men should do to you, do ye even so to them . . ." (Matthew 7:12).

We began to package our products in attractive, sturdy, boxes that protect their contents during shipping and on the shelf. These boxes are also reclosable and self-locking so the customer can examine the unit before purchasing it. The typical jobber, who is supplied by the warehouse distributor, offers a complicated and sophisticated service, considering they have to carry parts for hundreds of different model cars and trucks from American and foreign manufacturers on the road today.

Picture this scenario.

A salesperson, John Brown, is desperate. The brakes on his Buick LeSabre sedan have gone bad in Iowa while calling on customers. He is 700 miles from home with appointments waiting. He drives into a service garage where the mechanic finds he needs to replace the master cylinder.

"Can it be fixed today?" asks John Brown.

"If we can get a replacement," is the answer.

The mechanic calls the jobber who checks his inventory. Yes, they have a replacement. Someone from the garage picks it up and by noon John Brown is back on the road.

But take the case of Betty Taylor who delivers Meals on Wheels to shut-ins in Westchester County, New York. On the day before she's due to go out on her route, the power-steering pump on her Ford Tempo fails. The service manager shakes his head ruefully. "Our jobber doesn't have the part in stock," he says. "It may be three days before he gets it in, possibly longer."

"But I need the car tomorrow. What can I do?"

"I'm sorry" is all the mechanic can say.

If Betty Taylor can't borrow someone else's car, eleven shut-ins could miss their meals that day. To avoid problems like this, jobbers make it their business to keep full inventories. Thus when a warehouse distributor ships a partial order, it's enough to turn a jobber's hair gray.

That's why, from the start, we've always endeavored to ship our warehouse distributors 100 percent of all orders. Whether it was my wife, Fran, in the early days running to the post office to send a customer two wiper motors by special delivery or present-day employees fighting their way to the plant through a blizzard to keep our assembly lines going, we have prided ourselves on seeing that the warehouse distributor gets what he needs on time.

In his early days with us John Tedesco took some novel approaches in convincing customers we meant business with our fulfillment promise.

"I may have rushed in where angels fear to tread," he laughs today recalling it, "but I could see no other way. I was so intent on selling one distributor, I found myself promising, 'If we backorder just *one piece* on your shipment, I'll give you the entire order free.'

"The gleam in the man's eye almost blinded me," said John, "and he ordered three times his usual amount.

"He was used to shipments from other suppliers coming in full of back orders. It was the largest order I had ever written.

"Outside in my car a cold chill came over me when I realized what I had done. Even though I knew my company would back up my promise if we couldn't fill his order completely, I felt personally obligated to pay for it myself.

"But I remembered that old saying, 'Pray as if everything depended on God, and work as if everything depended on you.' I did both. Back at the plant I packed that order and shipped it myself."

But that little bit of dramatics resulted in an account who is one of our best customers today.

In trying to make the warehouse distributors' lives easier we've developed other new marketing services. Warehouse distributors and jobbers constantly face the problem of limited shelf space. Yet it's in their best interest to carry stocks of the most popular items. This can pose a problem in view of the many thousands of different replacement parts available.

To help them, our sales department came up with a "jobber mini-pack," a standardized shipment of selected items to assure them having the most wanted parts on hand. We have also consolidated parts numbers, giving the dealer maximum coverage with less inventory. For example, twelve of our distributors give the dealer 70 percent coverage.

Another customer headache was the complicated bookwork in ordering and pricing the thousands of differently priced parts. To help ease this task, we pioneered a one-price charge for each product line. For example, all our distributors, whether for GM, Chrysler, Ford, or other makes, would be priced the same.

By the same token, we led the way in instituting the one-price core deposit to simplify returns. Throughout the history of auto parts remanufacturing, it has been standard to include the deposit in the price of an item. This amount is reimbursed to the customer when he returns an old part in ordering a new one. Again, keeping track of the varying deposits among the thousands of parts was a real bookkeeping chore for everyone.

From our first day in business, we standardized our core deposit charge. For example, the deposit for practically all master cylinders was five dollars, no matter what make or model. When we received the core from the customer, he or she would be instantly reimbursed. We can do this because as soon as the cores arrive, we sort, count, and process them for remanufacturing.

The above innovations helped simplify ordering and bookwork for both the customer and us. Of course, it cost us more but in the long run our increasing number of satisfied customers more than made up for it.

We also have a high priority customer-service department with toll-free phones for orders. Marketing aids, such as advertising in major trade journals, are being continually developed to build customers' sales.

To supplement our own salespeople, we began putting on sales representatives in the early 1970s. Walter Sullivan was our first rep and he began calling on customers in the northeastern states. As of this writing, we have 100 sales reps and have expanded our marketing area nationwide.

To insure practically 100 percent availability on a forty-eight-hour basis to our national distribution network, we have distribution centers in Los Angeles, Houston, and Minneapolis that are served by our headquarters in Philadelphia.

In 1978 we bought our first truck, a GMC cab-over-engine tractor trailer. Gale Pettygrove was our first driver and we all gathered around the shiny cab to dedicate it to the Lord. As we prayed for the safety of its driver, I couldn't help but think of the old 1927 Model A Ford in which I delivered my first orders. Today, 25 state-of-the-art tractor trailer units bearing our name are on the road every day delivering parts on almost 100 percent availability on a forty-eight-hour basis.

As with the first truck, each one was dedicated to the Lord by our chaplains. And God has protected them. Those vehicles today cover 1.5 million miles a year, so far without a serious accident. There have been many close calls. One truck caught a heavy steel manhole cover between its dual rear wheels without damage or injury. Another time a heavy metal crank-handle dislodged from another truck came crashing through the windshield of one of our vehicles missing the driver by inches.

In November 1987 shortly after one of our trucks left Philadelphia for Maryland, word came to headquarters that a violent freak blizzard was swooping down on the Northeast Atlantic seaboard. Linda Hess, Director of Transportation, immediately tried to reach our driver on the CB to call him back but to no avail.

She felt a heaviness on her spirit for his safety and soon a number of us were praying for the driver. Several hours later he finally managed to reach a motel after battling drifts in white-out conditions.

When he called Linda to say he was safe, she gasped, "Thank God, we've all been praying for you."

"That's the only reason I got here all right," he said.

Our truck drivers have the option if they wish of using mud flaps, the kind that hang over the rear wheels, imprinted with "Jesus is Lord." These have proven to be a witness, also.

"A fellow sat down next to me at a truck stop luncheon counter and started talking," said one of our drivers. "Soon he began talking about his troubles and before we parted, I was able to lead him to the One who could help him. As we walked out of the restaurant together, I asked him how come he picked me to talk to and he said, 'It was those words on your mud flaps.'"

Another driver asked for a set of these mud flaps because he felt it helped him be extra courteous. "With those on my truck, the last thing you want to do is cut somebody off." Each year our drivers attend a "Truckers Retreat" that we sponsor for them and their families so they can get together in a truly recreational atmosphere.

Our volume is such that we often have to use other trucking companies in addition to our own transportation. We supply, for example, auto parts to such chains as Auto Zone, Pep Boys, and Nationwide, plus other remanufacturers who buy our parts and sell them under their own name to expand their own line. And though we pray for everyone connected with our business, outside trucking firms have occasionally had accidents.

One happened in 1983 when a trucking firm's tractor-trailer loaded with A-1 master cylinders was traveling down a highway in North Carolina and the trailer collapsed, splitting open and spilling some of its cargo onto the highway. As soon as we heard about it, we packed and shipped a duplicate order to our customer that same day and sent a crew out to help retrieve the cargo.

Since the packing cases were hardly bruised and most looked untouched, an acquaintance wondered why we didn't simply load them on another truck and send them on to the customer. After all, it was freight on board and legally belonged to the customer.

Instead, we brought the parts back to the plant where each item was unpacked and retested to make sure it was perfect.

"We couldn't take that chance," was all I could say. I could have added that though our customer would probably not have known the difference, the Lord would.

A truck accident is one thing, but an earthquake is another. When a major earthquake struck Los Angeles on Thursday, October 1, 1987, our entire distributing center near the quake's epicenter was put out of commission. Sam Hernandez, Vice-President of Distribution, grabbed a plane for Los Angeles that night and was at the warehouse Friday morning.

He faced a frightful sight. Shelves were collapsed, light fixtures were broken, and there was no electric power, elevator service, or water. It was estimated that it would take a week before we could begin shipping. After some intensive prayer, Sam and the warehouse staff went to work cleaning up the mess and collecting and testing parts to make sure they weren't damaged.

They needed more help and found it. Employees of some of the other firms that shared space in the same public warehouse had arrived on the scene but, not given any direction, were just sitting around. Sam Hernandez put them to work. The team worked far into the night using flashlights and by late Friday, 70 percent of the cleanup was completed. With Saturday as another day of work, their goal was to be operational by Monday morning. On Sunday morning, however, a heavy aftershock struck causing further damage. By Monday we were again shipping to customers from our Los Angeles plant.

What happened to customers' orders on that Friday when the warehouse was out of commission? We shipped them direct from our Philadelphia plant. It took some doing and cost us extra but kept the pipelines open to our customers.

Sam Hernandez, who used to be a pastor of Faith Temple in St. Paul, Minnesota, before coming with us, said that getting the warehouse back in operation in that short time was humanly impossible. But he and the others knew where to find their real help.

I am convinced more than ever that God is there with us in all the little things, like inspiring us to go the extra mile in delivering an order. For example, when Chicago was shut down by a blizzard, our truck transporting an order for a Windy City customer could get no closer than Gary, Indiana. Rather than deliver it sometime later on the next scheduled run, the driver unloaded the merchandise at a Gary warehouse and the minute the roads were opened, we rushed it direct to the customer by private carrier at our own cost.

Little things—like the incentive to instantly honor warranties without fuss or question and like helping us discern a needed improvement in a remanufactured product—reflect His presence. For example, the rack-and-pinion steering control unit that we began to remanufacture had a part we discovered was susceptible to corrosive elements such as road salt and chemicals. As a result, it pitted easily. To correct this condition, we designed a special steel sleeve to protect this part and installed it on all remanufactured units. As we like to say, the unit was "better than new."

Early in 1985 we entered the new world of automotive electronics. Again this was a case of being guided, I believe, to a need that had to be filled.

The average driver probably does not understand the electronic engine control computer that is part of most of today's new cars. This is a computer unit about the size of a cigar box that controls and monitors many important functions on a vehicle from fuel injection and piston firing to keeping watch over the emissions control system. These engine control computers are truly a space age development.

But just as things can go wrong with a space rocket, malfunctions can also develop in the control computers. But what does one do with one that fails? Crammed with resistors, diodes, and printed circuits, it would seem far simpler to discard rather than try to repair it. But new ones are expensive.

My son, Michael, and Joe Beretta, Vice-President of Engineering, were discussing the possibilities of remanufacturing these in 1985 but the outlook was bleak. In the first place manufacturers of new ones had enough to do without attempting to teach us how to remanufacture them. After seeking God's guidance, our engineers went to work. This was brought home to me one day when I picked up one of their pieces of complicated lab equipment to find on it the words, "Pray before using."

Our men started off doing what is called "reverse engineering." This means studying the engine control computer's function in minute detail by delicately disassembling the unit in the reverse order of its assembly. A young boy does this when he wants to know how a key-wound toy car works. He knows the wheels are powered so he takes them off, removes the axle and the gear that turns it, and continues until he finds the spring that powers it.

After eight months of intensive study, our engineers not only could build an engine control computer but knew what could go wrong with it, such as the wear of thermocycling, the heating up and cooling off of the components. Thus they learned how to remanufacture one and then to test it conclusively so it was "as good as new or better."

"How do you test a remanufactured engine control computer?" I asked Michael. "C'mon, Dad, I'll show you," he said. As I followed him through the plant, I remembered the little boy who learned how to take apart and reassemble the lawn mower carburetor on our kitchen table. Now he was Chief Executive Officer of M. Cardone Industries, Inc., responsible for its daily operations. I sensed the baton of leadership being passed from father to son. Michael brought me over to a strange-looking machine our lab had built. "It's a special computer, Dad, that duplicates all the functions of an auto. For example, while testing an engine control computer on it, we can simulate a bad fuel injector and if the unit is working properly, the testing device will signal this to its "dashboard" control panel just like the one in your car."

As I stood watching the blinking lights on the computerized test machine, I couldn't help but think of my old trial-and-error testing method on the vacuum windshield wiper motors I rebuilt in Bonney's garage.

As Michael adjusted the controls on the humming machine to test another function of the engine control computer, I sighed, "It looks like something from the twenty-first century."

Michael looked at me, and grinned. "Dad, it almost *is* the twenty-first century and we're taking M. Cardone Industries, Inc., right into it."

"Points to Remember"

(1) Take everything to the Lord in prayer and you will be overwhelmed at His response.
(2) Customer satisfaction is produced by quality, service, and availability.

Twelve

Road Warriors

Engine-control computers ... electronic testing ... It all whirled through my mind as I walked back to my office thinking how far remanufacturing had come since I took apart that first vacuum windshield wiper in Bonney's garage.

Then, as I sat down at my desk and picked up a batch of letters from a special group of men, I realized that one thing had not changed. And that was the help of the men who wrote me these letters. They were our sales representatives, our "road warriors." Though not company employees, they are vitally important to our success.

They are independent agents who work on the road, marketing our products to our customers. Most of them have been with us since the beginning and without their help we could not have grown to what we are today.

I rolled their names over in my mind. Walter Sullivan and his son, Dave, of the Sullivan Agency Northeast in Guilford, Connecticut; George Rayburn, together with his son-in-law, Don Odom, president of ROK & Associates of Dallas, Texas; Ray Palmaccio of Universal Sales in Philadelphia; Jack Kotter of Fraser, Michigan; Peter Valentine of Florida; Arnie Cohen of Illinois; and Norm Munze of Kansas.

Most of them had recently written me, recalling memories of the "old days." As I sat at my desk reading through their letters, I couldn't help but chuckle and sometimes break out in a hearty laugh.

Like Don Odom, reminding me of our "Rinky-Dink" days.

"In my seventeen years' association with A-1 Remanufacturing there is one incident I'll never forget," wrote Don. "It took place between my former partner, George Rayburn, and Michael Cardone, Sr., in 1974 at the ASIA Trade Show.

"Mike Cardone, as always, was seeking more sales and wanted to know what was wrong with A-1 products. George, who never handled criticism well, wasn't exactly himself that night. A hot discussion ensued which was climaxed when George stated loudly that ROK (our sales agency) was selling a lot of products, considering Cardone's "rinky-dink" line. I thank the Lord that Mike knew we were a good sales organization and was nice enough to forgive a few transgressions.

"After a successful career, George retired in 1980. However, Mike, his son, Michael, Jr., plus Peter Calo and John Tedesco in good-natured kidding never let us folks at ROK forget the "rinky-dink" line. Frankly, I'll never forget it either.

"The real climax to the whole thing came in 1987 when Michael Cardone, Sr., honored George Rayburn and his wife at a dinner meeting in Atlanta. The recognition thrilled George and the first-class travel certificate to Hong Kong Mike presented to him was the icing on the cake."

I smiled, remembering how, despite hot exchanges, men can remain warm friends when they relate in God's loving spirit.

Walter Sullivan will never forget his anxiety when he introduced a prospect to our little company back in our early days. He had taken his prospect, Lou Nulman of Alden Autoparts Warehouse, in a cab from the Philadelphia airport to our storefront building in northeast Philadelphia.

"It turned out to be a row house and my heart began to sink," wrote Walter. "I remember holding a flashlight as we picked our way down dark stairs to the cellar and warning Lou not to bump his head on the low stairway ceiling.

"The quizzical look on my prospect's face seemed to ask: 'What have I gotten into?'," continued Walter. "And I felt sure that in no possible way was I going to write an initial order.

"In the cellar, Michael, Sr., and another gentleman were working on wiper motors, distributors, and power-steering pumps. Mrs. Cardone stepped out of the tiny office to greet us. I could hardly believe it when I found out that she actually wrote the company's invoices by hand!

"Despite my trepidation, Lou Nulman was so charmed by Frances and Michael that he told me to write up an initial order on the different products.

"'You know,' said Lou to me after we left, 'I admire that man for his courage in starting a new business in his fifty-fifth year.'

"But," wrote Walter, "it was more than courage that impressed Lou. He saw that Michael had a vision that would not be denied."

As I read Walter Sullivan's letter, I remembered that meeting with Lou Nulman very well. Today, his Alden Autoparts Warehouse is one of our largest customers.

Walter's son, Dave, joined his father in his business the same year my son, Michael, Jr., joined me in mine. Dave wrote of an experience similar to his father's when he came to visit our little shop.

"Expecting to find a large plant, I had taken the liberty of bringing a prospective customer, planning to impress him. What we found, instead, was a small room staffed with Mr. and Mrs. Cardone, Michael, and only one or two others. I was shocked and wondered what my prospect was thinking.

"It turned out he was so favorably impressed by the Cardones and the excellent product that I soon found myself—in somewhat of a daze—writing up his order. Needless to say I went on to write up quite a few more orders and today we are a top sales agency.

"I learned that day," continued Dave, "that it's not the size of the factory that's important to a customer, but the integrity of the people who run it and the quality of the product they produce."

And then I picked up a letter from Sales Rep Ray Palmaccio who never forgot the times when I wouldn't take his advice.

"And I'm glad he didn't," Ray wrote.

"Back in the late sixties when Mike Cardone told me he was interested in going into his own remanufacturing business and asked my opinion about rebuilding distributors and wiper motors, my answer was: 'Save your money. Nobody buys these items.'

"Later, he asked my opinion about power steering, blower motors, and master cylinders. Again my answer was: 'Save your money.' And, again he proved me wrong. Afterward, I learned that many other people had given him the same opinion.

"But thank goodness, Mike had the vision, determination, and knowledge that proved all of us wrong. I'm grateful I was his first salesman.

"But, in a way," concluded Ray, "Michael Cardone, Sr., was wrong, too. For I don't believe in all his wildest dreams did he ever think he would have accomplished all that he has."

Ray was right on that one.

The next letter was from a man who had no idea we'd be working together when we first met.

"Sixteen years ago I was doing private contracting work for Michael Cardone when he first moved into Plant Number One on American Street," wrote Peter Valentine, M. Cardone Industries Regional Sales Manager for the state of Florida. "He approached me about the possibility of air-conditioning his plant. We finally came up with the financing and the work was completed, making it the only remanufacturing plant in the country at that time to be fully air-conditioned.

"After this project was completed, I decided to sell my business and move to Florida. When Mr. Cardone heard of my plans, he approached me with the possibility of working for him as a sales representative in Florida as he had no representation in that state at that time since it then had only one automotive-warehouse distributor.

"I told him I'd give it a shot. And I began traveling Florida trying to sell his Mini-Pack Distributors which, at that time, was our main product. It was very hard work and discouraging trying to sell a product that no warehouse manager wanted. I was about to throw in the towel but then got the idea of going to the jobber stores and selling *them* the Mini Pack. When I took their orders back to the warehouse distributors, they couldn't turn down our product.

"Since then it has been exciting to see how the Lord has blessed our efforts. Now we have over fifty warehouse distributors in Florida."

I visualized Peter Valentine plugging away day after day to convince his customers of his product's worth by selling *their* customers, much like what our John Tedesco did in his early days.

Then Jack Kotter of Michigan recalled his starting with us in 1973 when we wrapped our products in newspapers, ". . . a far cry from M. Cardone's modern sophisticated packaging of today," he wrote. "However, one element in all this has not changed," he added, "the emphasis on quality the Cardones place on each and every product."

As I put the packet of letters down with a warm heart, I remembered a statement attributed to Henry Ford back in the thirties who said he had good engineers to make his cars but was always looking for crackerjack salesmen to sell them.

Thank God, I thought, for our excellent engineers who put the quality in our A-1 Remanufactured auto parts, and thank God for our sales reps who sell them. They make a great team.

"Points to Remember"

(1) Our God is a God through good times and bad; when the crisis is worst, our faith can be strongest and God accomplishes His greatest miracles.
(2) In our prayers we should be specific in expressing our needs.

Thirteen

Ryan's Miracle

It was April 1, 1979, and Frances and I were entertaining a family gathering when the call came. We had been anxiously awaiting it ever since our son had taken his wife, Jacquie, to the hospital for the birth of their third child. Several hours had passed and we were becoming concerned. Jacquie usually had her children sooner than this.

Before the phone rang, Frances had turned to me and quietly confided, "I'm worried, Mike."

"Everything's going to be all right, Fran," I soothed. "It's probably taking longer than anyone thought." I lied, for I was worried too.

Then the phone rang. I leaped for it and gave thanks as I heard Michael's voice. "Michael, how's Jacquie?"

"It's a boy, Dad," he said. "His name is Ryan." The phone was quiet for a moment and then Michael added in a husky voice, "But there's a problem."

I gripped the phone. *Oh no, Lord,* I breathed silently.

"What's wrong?" I asked.

"Ryan has spina bifida," said Michael, explaining that it was a small opening at the base of his spine. I knew it was serious.

After a few more words, Michael hung up the phone as he was waiting to learn more from their doctor.

Needless to say, Frances and I did not sleep that night. We prayed for our new grandchild, for Jacquie and Michael. Later Michael told us their nerve-wracking story.

The doctor who had delivered their baby had immediately called their pediatrician. While Michael waited for him, he rushed to Jacquie's bedside. She smiled weakly as he leaned down to kiss her.

"They say something's wrong with Ryan," she said.

Michael gripped her hand. "Don't worry, honey," he said, "I'm sure it will work out all right."

After the pediatrician saw Ryan, he sat with Michael for a consultation. His face grave, he explained that Ryan had a condition in which several of the spinal vertebrae had failed to close completely, allowing the spinal cord and nerves in the area to bulge through the opening. There was an immediate danger of infection where the spinal cord was exposed and Ryan needed to be transferred to another hospital now. He recommended a neurosurgeon at St. Christopher's Children's Hospital, about twenty miles away.

Within an hour little Ryan, only two hours old, was in an ambulance being whisked to the hospital where the operation would be performed the next day, an operation that he might not survive.

Michael again phoned us and everyone else he could think of asking them to pray for their baby. He hardly slept that night and early the next morning he was at St. Christopher's waiting to see the neurosurgeon. He found himself pacing back and forth across the waiting room, his mind a boiling caldron of fears of what might happen to Ryan.

The neurosurgeon was late and the strain was becoming unbearable. Then he felt a hand on his shoulder and turned to find our pastor, Edward Menaldino, standing there. Turning to 2 Corinthians, chapter 10, Pastor Menaldino read verses 3 to 5: "For though we walk in the flesh, we do not war after the flesh: (For the weapons of our warfare are not carnal, but mighty through God to the pulling down of strong holds;) Casting down imaginations, and every high thing that exalteth itself against the knowledge of God, and bringing into captivity every thought to the obedience of Christ."

He looked up from his Bible at Michael. "Do you understand what He's telling us?"

Michael nodded. He knew that by itself his mind was subject to the negative spirits of the earth. But when he gave it to God, the Holy Spirit would control his imagination and fears and allow him to think sensibly and calmly.

Sinking down on the sofa, he relaxed into the loving arms of God, who was with Ryan. A new confidence flowed into Michael as he now felt that nothing could happen to Ryan that God would not allow.

However, his confidence was shaken again when he met the neurosurgeon. A calm, no-nonsense professional man, he frankly described Ryan's condition.

"Your son has a severe form of spina bifida," he said, taking out a medical textbook and turning to an illustration.

He explained that the spinal cord and nerves that normally control muscles and sensation in the bladder, bowels, and legs had bulged through the opening in the spinal column forming a fluid-filled sac protruding from Ryan's back.

"Because that sac, which we call a myelomeningocele, is only partially covered, the exposed nerves can be easily damaged and the risk of paralysis and infection is high," he further explained.

"What can we hope for after the operation?" Michael pressed.

The neurosurgeon put down the medical book and took a deep breath. "It might save his life, but. . . ."

Michael stared at him. "But what?"

"I'm sorry to have to tell you this, Mr. Cardone," the doctor continued, "but in all likelihood Ryan will never walk."

Michael sat back in his chair, breathing heavily. The room was still. He waited for the surgeon to continue.

He cleared his throat. "There's also the possibility of hydrocephalus," he added. He pointed out that this is where the spinal fluid becomes blocked and accumulates dangerously in the brain to where the head becomes enlarged. "Mental retardation usually results," he said.

"However, thank God, we can generally prevent that by surgically implanting a thin plastic tube in the brain. The excess fluid is shunted away through it and ultimately absorbed by the body."

By now Michael felt helpless. Ryan unable to walk? Plastic tubes in his brain? Future operations indefinitely? He found himself floundering and again reached out for the only one who could offer real help. And God did. Michael felt the strong presence of His Holy Spirit.

He had heard the worst. Now he wanted to know the best. As God's Spirit took control of his thoughts, he pressed the doctors for detailed information on each problem they had presented. When they explained the situation in their terms, Michael insisted they also tell him the best that they could expect. Michael would expect their best and then pray for God to give Ryan His best beyond the doctors' ability.

"What are the best probabilities you see for Ryan, Doctor?" he asked. "What can you do for him?"

"Well," he said, his voice taking on a more optimistic tone, "I do see that he has roughly seventy percent leg movement, but that won't be enough for him to walk without braces or orthopedic surgery.

"I'm sorry," he sighed, "I can't give you any better news than that; it's just that the nerves are probably severed, like a cut telephone cable."

Michael pressed him with question after question about Ryan's chances. He felt that all of us needed to start praying specifically for those areas where the doctor could not do anything. The possibility of an infection, for example. Michael knew we should begin praying about that. He mentioned this to the doctor.

"Good," he replied, "pray for these three things: first, that there be no infection; second, that his spinal damage be contained; and third, that hydrocephalus be minimal."

Michael felt a strong presence, a comforting, sustaining presence. He now realized that Ryan's condition wasn't his problem. It was the Lord's and he knew that God would take care of him.

"And we will pray for *you*, Doctor, as you perform the operation," he said quietly. The surgeon was silent for a moment and looked down. Raising his head, he looked at Michael. "Thank you, I'll really appreciate that."

Our son walked out of the surgeon's office feeling confident, feeling that now he could do something. And not only him, but everyone he could think of. He called us, all the family and friends, asking them to pray for those three things, asking God to work specifically in those areas.

Then he went back to the hospital to see Jacquie. Standing by her bed, looking at his wife smiling up at him, he choked up and fell to his knees beside her bed crying. Finally, he was able to tell her everything he had learned about their son.

Jacquie comforted him. "The Lord has given me a verse of Scripture, 'Trust in the Lord with all thine heart and lean not to thine own understanding.' We don't understand what's happening but the Lord wants us to trust Him. He's in control."

Together, they went to St. Christopher's intensive care unit to see their baby. It was a difficult thing to do. Little Ryan looked so perfect, laying there in his incubator, no sign of the deadly protrusion of his lower spine that was covered by a little white blanket. Again, a sense of God's presence came over them and Michael took Jacquie's hand as they watched their son sleeping peacefully.

"Honey," said Jacquie softly, "I just know that this is going to be for the Lord's glory."

Michael has told us that as he stood there at that moment he felt completely at peace for the first time that day. No one was telling them that Ryan was going to be completely healed, but they had been given a deep spiritual reassurance by the Lord. Now they were content, willing to accept whatever was going to happen because they felt that God had brought this baby to them for something special, that they were his chosen parents. Michael had ceased trying to reason everything out. Whether his son lived or not, all he knew was that Ryan, Jacquie, and he were in God's hands, all part of His great plan.

The next day as the surgeons began working on their tiny son, Jacquie and Michael waited together. Despite the assurance given to him the previous night, his mind now raced with thoughts of what might happen. The spirit is willing but the flesh is so weak. He envisioned the surgeon coming toward them shaking his head, telling them that Ryan would never walk. His imagination leaped ahead to building wheelchair ramps throughout the house, to seeing Ryan sadly watching other boys play ball, seeing others do those things he would never do.

Heartsick, Michael reached for the Bible as a drowning man clutches at a life preserver. Flipping through the pages, he wondered what to read at a time like this. Then, not being led to any particular section, he turned to the book of Genesis. Why not begin at the beginning?

As he read about God forming the earth in six days, a question nagged at him. Why didn't He do it in one day? Then, just as if God had been waiting for him to ask that question, he answered, "The problem with Ryan is not going to go away in one day. This is going to be a gradual healing. We are going to take one day at a time, one miracle at a time."

Suddenly, like clouds being blown away from a mountaintop so that one could see the snowy peak shining in the sunlight, it became clear to Michael. God was telling him to focus his faith on the priority of the moment instead of spreading it over everything.

"Don't worry about a month, or even a week from now," God seemed to be telling him, "think about just today."

And the priority of today, of course, was Ryan's operation. Michael shared with Jacquie his illumination. She squeezed his hand and together they sat praying for the doctor, praying that his hands be guided by the Lord, and that angels would be standing at each corner of that operating table guarding Ryan.

As they waited, the minutes stretched into endless hours. Then the telephone broke the silence and Michael picked it up, his heart racing.

It was the surgeon. He sounded elated. "Mr. Cardone, I am delighted at what I saw on the inside of Ryan."

Michael's heart leaped. "Praise God!"

"For the size of the opening, I have never seen the spinal damage so contained," the doctor said. "It's very unusual," he added, "but isn't this what you were praying for?"

Michael smiled.

"Good," the doctor continued, "now pray that infection will not develop and that hydrocephalus doesn't develop. This is our most urgent concern."

Our most urgent concern. Well then, Michael reasoned, if they were to follow God's guidance on priorities, they would pray about this.

"When do you plan to operate again?" he asked the surgeon.

"Next week."

Michael took a deep breath. "Doctor, we are confident that you are not going to have to do this operation."

The surgeon paused for a long moment, then said, "I hope you're right."

From that day on, Jacquie and Michael prayed that the Holy Spirit would enter their little baby's body and find a passage for the fluid to flow around the spinal defect. They visualized it happening, picturing it in their minds, leaving Ryan completely in God's hands.

The following Monday he was wheeled into the X-ray room for a brain scan in preparation for the operation. After the X rays were viewed, the doctor found the young parents in the waiting room. He seemed to be awestruck. "Mr. Cardone," he began slowly, "I have seen something like this only one other time in my practice. But you are right; this baby is not going to need that operation."

In a few days Michael and Jacquie took our new grandson home. He seemed fine, but there was the big question about the nerve damage to his legs. They had certainly been affected. Every two weeks they took him to the neurosurgeon for an examination. He carefully tested Ryan's reactions, checking every aspect of his nervous system, measuring the flexing of his chubby little legs.

Finally, after several months, the doctor rested his hand on Ryan's little body, almost as a benediction, and shook his head. "I want you folks to know that I have had nothing to do with what has happened here. We cannot restore nerves; in fact, we usually cause more damage through handling them. But this little fellow's legs are moving better than before the surgery."

Jacquie and Michael looked at each other, both thinking of the same Scripture from Jeremiah 33:3: "Call unto me, and I will answer thee, and shew thee great and mighty things, which thou knowest not."

One year later, the same doctor examined Ryan again. "Your son has perfectly normal function in his legs," he told them. "In fact, he probably has better control than the average one-year-old."

Today, Ryan is a healthy, normal child. Every time we look into his bright and shining face, we know that God is a God for good times and for crisis. And I know that when the crisis is at its worst, that's when our faith can be strongest and God can do the greatest miracles of all.

All of us have learned that no matter how hopeless the crisis, God wants us to *pray for priorities*, not what may happen in the future, not what our frightened imaginations may conjure, but to pray for the problem facing us today.

"Evil is sufficient unto today," Jesus said, "give no thought for tomorrow."

As God healed Ryan one step at a time and we believe for His continuing touch in Ryan's body, we also seek to apply God's revelation to us for every other need in our lives. As my son, Michael, so dramatically discovered, we should focus our faith on the need of the moment.

The other day a tousled-haired young man stood in the doorway of my study at home. "Want to go swimming, Grandpa?"

"Sure do," I said, "I'll race you to the pool." As I watched Ryan's tanned stalwart legs flash in the sun, I gave thanks that our God, through His Son, Jesus Christ, is the One who said, "Suffer the little children and let them come unto me."

"Points to Remember"

(1) When we focus our attention on the Lord, and not our problems, He always sustains us.
(2) God's grace is more than enough to see us through the worst times.

Fourteen

A Celebration of Healing

I'll never forget that Wednesday morning in the fall of 1986. A minor glitch had developed on the fuel-pump assembly line and Mark Spuler, our Executive Vice-President, and I were working with other technicians on it. We had just about zeroed in on the problem when our factory public-address system boomed out my name.

"Mr. Cardone, please call the operator."

Shaking my head at the interruption, I stepped over to the post-mounted phone and picked it up. The operator said: "Mr. Cardone, your wife called. She's not feeling well at all and needs you at home."

My heart hammering, I waved at Mark and the others and rushed out to my car in the parking lot. While driving home I berated myself for leaving Fran at all this morning. She had been complaining of some pains the last few days but we both thought it was something that would pass. This morning she looked more troubled than ever but shrugged it off, waving me on to work.

"Go on, Mike," she urged, "I'll be all right."

As I kissed her good-bye, she smiled and said lightly, "Just pray for me, OK?"

I had, asking the Lord to give Fran relief as I drove to the plant that morning and again as our supervisors and I gathered for devotions. But, as too often happens in the press of handling phone calls, going over reports, and getting involved in the assembly line glitch, it had passed my mind.

Now as I sped toward home along roads flecked with yellow fallen leaves, I found myself praying desperately, asking our Father through His Son, Jesus Christ, to ease Fran's pain, to heal whatever was bothering her.

Our housekeeper, Minnie, met me at the door, her face pale. "Mrs. Cardone is upstairs," she quavered.

In our bedroom I found Fran on the bed moaning. She took my hand. "It hurts here, Mike," she said, laying it on her abdomen.

I picked up the phone and called her physician, Dr. Creech, who said he'd have an ambulance at the house right away.

"I'll meet you at the hospital," he added.

Soon an ambulance swerved into our drive, two medics leaped out and got a stretcher, and I ushered them into the bedroom. They eased Fran onto the stretcher, hurried her into the ambulance, and closed the door, and while one started taking her blood pressure, I climbed into the front seat.

With siren wailing, we sped toward Jeannes Hospital as I

stared dazedly out the windshield thinking how quickly things can change. This morning Fran and I had been looking forward to a get-together with the children celebrating the opening of our grandson Eric's carburetor rebuilding business. He was following in the footsteps of his father, Ruben Tarno, Ruth's husband, who owned his own rebuilding firm, Crown Remanufacturing, the one he had started after helping us get going in our early days. Fran and Minnie had been planning the menu this morning. Now everything had changed; I couldn't help but remember the Apostle Paul's answer to those who asked when the Lord would return again: "For yourselves know perfectly that the day of the Lord so cometh as a thief in the night" (1 Thessalonians 5:2).

As I thought of how our lives can change so unexpectedly, I realized more than ever the importance of keeping constantly in His presence. For only through the abiding presence of Jesus Christ, can we face tribulations.

The ambulance pulled up to the emergency room entrance and Fran was rushed into the examining room where Dr. Creech waited. Within a few hours Fran was being wheeled to surgery. In the hall I leaned down and kissed her wan face. She smiled weakly up at me, showed me a little red Gideon Bible someone had just given her, and whispered, "It's here, Mike, Psalms 16:1 . . . I'm holding on to it." While I sat anxiously in the waiting lounge with our son and daughter, I opened my own Bible to that psalm and read, "Preserve me, O God: for in thee do I put my trust."

As time went on, I thought of the dichotomy we humans experience, the kind I was going through right now. On one hand our "old man," the carnal side of our nature, lives in constant fear of the unknown. On the other our renewed spirit in Christ abides in Him, fearless, trusting. But, as a believer, we make that choice and I abided in Him.

"Mr. Cardone?"

I looked up. It was Dr. Creech. "Your wife is fine; I thought we were facing something serious but it was a small bit of surgery we had to do and she'll be up and around shortly."

"Thank you," I sighed, feeling a heavy load slide off my back.

"We're going to keep her a few days so I can give her a complete examination," he added.

"Fine, doctor."

Two days later I met Dr. Creech in his office; his face was serious.

"I'm sorry, Mr. Cardone, but we don't have good news."

I looked up in surprise. "I thought. . . ."

"No, it's not what brought her in here," he said, breaking in. "It is what we've found in the examination."

He cleared his throat, and continued. "We put your wife through a body CAT scan and. . . ."

I leaned forward.

"We discovered a tumor on her lung."

The office walls seemed to fall in on me.

He turned to the wall and flicked on a light. There illuminated from behind were X rays of Fran's lungs. Dr. Creech pointed to a dark spot in the left one.

"It's about the size of a fifty-cent piece and. . . ."

"Cancer?" I asked in a pained voice.

He turned off the light and sat down at his desk. He looked down at the pen he was twisting in his hand. "It could be," he said slowly. Then he looked up. "But right now we don't really know. For the time being I believe we should watch it."

"But she's never smoked, doctor," I said, pleadingly as if that statement would remove the danger.

He shook his head. "We never know what starts these things. All we can do is wait and see."

When Fran returned home I cautioned her to take it easy.

"Now don't worry, Mike," she said. "I know what I can and cannot do." She seemed at peace and went about her usual activities, cooking, doing my secretarial work, and keeping track of our tithing, something she had done since our marriage.

Dr. Creech had given her medication to take regularly. "I know God heals," she said, "and I know He works through good doctors, too."

All the same I worried. I watched her closely and seemed to see a fatigue in her face that hadn't been there before.

For the first time in our forty-five years of marriage I realized I could lose Fran.

The thought filled me with dread; I couldn't shake it as I worked, as I visited with the family. As I drove to the plant, my mind would go back to those early days when Fran accompanied me in the Model A while I delivered wiper motors. I smiled remembering her being my "watcher," standing guard over our deliveries to keep them safe while I returned to the car for more. I remembered her pert chin held high, her sparkling brown eyes defying any thief, our treats afterward at an ice-cream parlor sharing a chocolate milk shake or hot fudge sundaes.

Then I remembered the verse Fran had clung to, "Preserve me God . . . for in thee do I put my trust." Again, I realized I had that choice: to let myself go on worrying, or turn to Him.

And so I relinquished Fran. "Father, I give You my wife. I know You are the great Physician, the great Healer. I know You want the best for her. In Thee I put my trust."

A deep peace came over me and when I told Fran that I had been able to do this, she smiled, "Mike, I did that right after Dr. Creech told me."

In the meantime, everyone was praying for Fran, our

church and minister, all our employees, friends, and every prayer group I could think of. All were storming heaven, including the people at *Guideposts* magazine whose staff pray every Monday morning at 9:45 for those who request it.

It seemed I could actually feel the strength of those prayers, a sustaining presence uplifting us. I asked Fran if she felt the same way and she nodded emphatically. "What do you think has been helping me keep my head on straight?" she said. I leaned over and kissed her.

Before we realized it, Fran was scheduled for her next visit with Dr. Creech. He said he would take X rays. "Judging from how much it has grown will tell us a lot more," he said.

As the day neared, Fran maintained her usual cheerfulness. My own apprehension began to return. But I knew that its source, Satan, is constantly trying to get us to give up hope in God. Our daughter, Ruth, went with her. Ruth had been such a comfort to us through the years. And now she was staying especially close to her mother, blessing her with that companionship only a daughter can provide. I had wanted to go with them, too, but Fran discouraged me saying, "You know how it is in the doctor's office, all that time wasted waiting."

I suspect she thought I'd get too nervous, that I'd be better off occupied with work. Although I was worried, I continued remembering that He was a God of miracles. I returned home from the plant early that day to pace the living room. As I passed the bookshelves, I picked up the little brass carburetor young Mike and I had worked on so long ago. I remembered the two of us hunched over it at the kitchen table, Fran doing the dishes, coming over occasionally to see how we were doing.

I heard the key in the door. I rushed to it and met her as she stepped into the house. I looked into her eyes questioningly.

She smiled. "Mike, it hasn't grown; maybe it's a little smaller."

I gave a big sigh. "Praise God!"

Fran took off her coat and sat down. "Dr. Creech still can't make any promises. Right now we don't know. I have to go back again in two months."

Could I stand those two months? Fran's condition occupied my thoughts more and more. Her spirits remained high and she continued day in and day out cheerfully.

I began to appreciate all the more God's gift of married love. I was so grateful for our years we had together. As I watched the growing number of divorces, of people "living together" without a commitment, I grieved for them. What they were missing! I looked back on our forty-five years of marriage, the joys, the pain we shared. Like all couples we had our arguments; I could be bullheaded and Fran could spark back, too. But always we had talked over our differences, had prayed together, and had not, as the Bible admonished, "let the sun go down on our anger." Now our treasure was our children and grandchildren.

"Oh Lord," I prayed, "Fran and I have so much living yet to do in serving You. Please keep us together."

Fran's second visit to Dr. Creech took place around Christmas and brought us more amazing news. The tumor was getting smaller. What a wonderful Christmas gift!

"It could change," he said, warning us not to have false hope. "We really don't know about these things."

And so we continued praying.

Two more months passed and the third visit brought news that it was even smaller. February's snow was heaped high outside but it was spring in my heart.

"I really don't know," said the doctor. "It's still there, however, and we'll just have to watch it."

In April, six months after we had been given the dreaded news, Fran was due for her fourth visit. I felt this would be a crucial one. Again I waited. I had wanted to go with Fran but again she felt I'd be better off home. Was there something she had heard, I wondered, that she wasn't telling me?

I stepped out into our backyard. It was warm under the April sun and I looked at the flowers Fran had so carefully nurtured. Would she be tending them again this summer? I heard our car in the drive and rushed into the house to the front door and pulled it open. Fran threw her arms around me, crying, "Mike, it's gone!"

I could hardly believe her.

"Gone?" I echoed.

"Gone!" she repeated. "Praise the Lord! Praise the Lord! Praise the Lord!" she exclaimed, throwing her hands in the air. I grabbed her in my arms and we did a little dance around the living room. On catching our breath, we sat down and Fran told me what happened.

"He showed me the X rays, Mike, and pointed to the spot where the tumor was. It had completely vanished!

"He had Ruth look too. And she saw it had gone, also."

Ruth nodded happily.

"Why? How come?" I asked.

"He said that of all his patients with tumors who had taken my same medication, only one other woman and I had this happen."

She laughed. "Of course, I told him only the Lord could have done that!"

To celebrate Fran's healing, we had a party and invited all my brothers and sisters with their families.

That evening as we prepared to sit down to dinner, I looked at my family and thought back to how we had all started out together in Hughestown, how we had picked huckleberries, worked our paper and delivery routes, walked to that little Pentecostal church, and found the Lord. And now, here we were, celebrating a miracle together.

God was so good.

I looked at Fran seated at the other end of the table and caught her eye. She smiled and it seemed just like that time we first met so many years ago.

Yes, there was love in that room, family love, marital love, godly love, all the wonderful gifts with which He blesses us when we trust and obey.

In giving thanks to Him I felt such a faith in His promises. Of course, I knew other illnesses would come, other troubles would afflict us. But I also knew that whatever came, He would be there, sustaining us, uplifting us, guiding us, until He welcomed us home.

I raised my glass to Fran. "To our guest of honor."

She never looked more beautiful.

"Points to Remember"

(1) God's gift of marital love is a priceless treasure. God blesses those marriages that bless Him.
(2) God's healing power is available for us today.

Fifteen

A Look Ahead

Late one evening I was walking through the plant, as I sometimes do, in a quiet time of reflection. It was shut down for the night and the silent machines rested in pools of illumination from the night lights.

I had just come from a convention of automotive part remanufacturers and one of the subjects under discussion was employee loyalty and how a firm can maintain it. In many places this attribute doesn't seem to be so fashionable anymore.

As I mulled it over, I passed a work station with an old hammer on top. Well worn and obviously due for replacement, it brought back memories of another hammer that had been important in my life. It had belonged to an old man in Hughestown I remember as Mr. Grundini. A grouchy fellow who was somewhat of a hermit, he lived by himself in a hovel at the edge of town. Even though he was almost blind, his nasty temper had strained the patience of most everyone in town and he was generally left alone. Occasionally he would do odd carpentry jobs for people such as repair a stoop or fix a stuck door. This was when his most cherished possessions came to light, his tools. Before commencing work, he would carefully unwrap them from an old cloth and lay them out the way a surgeon arranges his instruments. They were old but of extremely high quality and well cared for. Some of the carpenters in town had offered to buy some of them but he would fiercely shake his head. They were the one thing in his life that seemed to give it some meaning. Children would taunt him from a distance and then run screaming when he turned and shuffled toward them. Some of the older boys would throw crabapples at him.

One evening as I walked home along the railroad tracks, I almost stumbled on him. He was hunched over picking up pieces of coal from between the ties. He looked up at me, his rheumy eyes filled with fear.

I hesitated and was about to walk on around him when something stopped me. Perhaps it was the apprehension in his face. By then I had already met the Lord and I discerned the loneliness and emptiness in his life. Why was he so alone? What had happened to his family?

On impulse I bent down and helped him fill his gunnysack with pieces of the gritty anthracite laying on the gravel. He stared at me in surprise, then mumbling something, he hoisted the sack on his shoulder and shuffled toward his shack.

From then on I would occasionally leave a sack of coal by his door. Coal was an obtainable commodity in Hughestown if one knew where to look. There were always places where it had spilled off trucks and loading chutes; an energetic youngster could easily fill a sackful. That's how I got my hair cut for years: A bag of coal to feed our barber's ever-hungry potbellied stove was always worth a trim.

When other youngsters, who thought the only coal worth delivering to Mr. Grundini was a well-aimed shard, found out what I was doing, I was ridiculed. But it didn't bother me. By then I was learning how good one felt when going out of one's way for another. As Jesus said, "Whosoever shall give to drink unto one of these little ones a cup of cold water . . . he shall in no wise lose his reward" (Matthew 10:42).

Mr. Grundini never made it a point to thank me. He either was not home or incommunicado when I'd leave the coal at his door. And the few times I'd see him on the street he'd trudge by wordlessly, grimy coat flapping in the wind, tattered slouch hat pulled down over his eyes. But that didn't bother me either.

However, just before I left for Philadelphia, he waved me over on the street one day. My first impulse was to hurry on, but there was something insistent about his wave. Reluctantly I crossed over to him. As I stared questioningly at him, he rummaged around within his coat and pulled out a hammer which he thrust at me.

I sensed a finely balanced craftsman's instrument. Its ash handle was smooth and shiny from years of use and its head had obviously driven home carloads of nails. Clearly, it was Mr. Grundini's cherished possession.

I looked into his faded brown eyes. "No, Mr. Grundini," I said, pushing the hammer back at him, "I can't take this . . . You don't have to. . . ."

"Si, si," he rasped, "you good boy, take with you to Philadelphia. It bring luck."

His gnarled fingers pressed mine as he placed the hammer back in my hands.

"Vai con Dio," he said, then turned and trudged off.

I stood watching him as he disappeared in the shadows, a lump filling my throat. It was then I realized it wasn't so much the coal Mr. Grundini appreciated, but that I had gone out of my way for him.

I did take that hammer with me to Philadelphia and used it for years, from remanufacturing those first vacuum windshield wiper motors in Bonney's garage to starting my little shop in Grandma Mark's basement. I don't know about the hammer bringing me luck, but more important, every time I used it, I sensed God's blessing.

More than a helpful tool, it was a constant reminder of what people treasure more than money, of being appreciated as a human being, of being valued as a child of God. This, I believe, is what builds true employee loyalty.

It is on this loyalty that the future of M. Cardone Industries rests, the some twelve hundred people who now staff our company, who receive the cores, who disassemble them, who remanufacture and test them, and who sell and deliver them throughout the world.

How long will our company continue? How much more will it grow? Only God has the answer.

All I know is that we who are responsible for its progress will continue taking up His cross. Where He leads, we will follow.

As a youngster I used to think that accepting the cross of Jesus meant tribulation, sorrow, and rejection. It can, and often does, I know from my own experience.

But in a greater sense taking up the cross means accepting God's will for one's life, no matter what His will may be. One thing I know: God's will is for His children to be happy. He wants us to be of service to Him and our fellowmen, to be contributing members of society.

In my case I feel God's will is for us to run our company so that we can best serve our customers and provide the greatest opportunities for our employees. We want each one to know that his or her well-being is more important than profits. To this end our prime rule of business is the one given by Jesus in Matthew 6:33: "But seek ye first the kingdom of God, and his righteousness; and all these things shall be added unto you."

Our statement of purpose is as follows:

1. Honor God in all we do.
2. Help people develop.
3. Pursue excellence.
4. Grow profitably.

Naturally, we are interested in making a profit for without it we couldn't pay our employees, invest in new equipment to keep our plants efficient, and maintain our ministries and missionary projects. But we are not in remanufacturing just to make money. If that were the case, we could have sold our business a number of times over and lived well on the proceeds. The truth is, we enjoy it too much to think about doing anything else.

I like to think that my own descendants and those of our employees will follow in my footsteps. Already my fourteen-year-old grandson, Michael Cardone III, works on engine control computers in our plant on summer vacations. I remember him as a ten-year-old helping clean the old cores as they came in, his hands and face black with grease, grinning from ear to ear. His sister Christin, age twelve, is already learning our telephone switchboard. And little Ryan, now a healthy ten-year-old, is eager to help where he can.

They and other children of our employees represent the future of our company, a future in which we see nothing but growth if we continue to seek the kingdom of God and His righteousness.

I love to walk through our plant whether during quiet after-work hours or the bustle of day. As I watch the old, worn-out, dirty cores come into our Core Division and then see the same piece of equipment leave the assembly line, brand new, shiny, and restored for service, I can't but help think of how God can take our lives, no matter how troubled and broken, and rebuild us into brand-new people. It is never too late.

After all, He is the Master Rebuilder.

"Points to Remember"

(1) Honor your employees and they will honor you.
(2) When you put God first, He will prosper you.

Sharing the Vision

The bright spring sun warming the fresh greens of the links was in complete contrast to the dark mood of my golfing partner. He had just scored a birdie on the 17th hole but instead of jubilating, the dark frown never left his face. I felt concern for him. A successful businessman with a growing family shouldn't look that worried, I thought. After we holed out on the 18th and toted up our scores, I patted his back. "Bill, with a great score like that you should be celebrating," I said. "Instead you look like you're facing six months of root canal work."

He laughed ruefully. "I wish it were as simple as that, Mike."

"What's wrong?"

Oh, you don't want to hear my troubles."

"Well, they say talking about your worries is one way to help get over them," I said. "Let's relax a moment at one of these umbrella tables and let me get you some refreshment."

Bill hesitated for a moment, glanced at his watch, then looked up. "Oh, I guess I can spare some time. I haven't been handling even that very well lately."

For two hours that afternoon Bill unloaded his worries. His business wasn't going too well, his older son had gotten in trouble with the police and he'd been putting off seeing a doctor about some physical problems.

Finally he leaned back in his chair and sighed. "Told you it would be boring, Mike."

I shook my head. "On the contrary, Bill, I've been through some deep waters myself, and I know what you're going through. Thank God I found help."

Bill leaned across the table. "That's what I've always wondered about," he said. "You always look so calm and collected. What's your secret? A good psychiatrist?"

I smiled. "No, someone far more helpful."

"Who is that?"

"The Lord, Bill. I don't know what I'd do without Him."

Bill slumped back in his chair. "Oh," he sighed, " that... I thought you were going to tell me where I could find some real help."

"Don't you believe in Him?"

"Oh sure," he said, looking out over the fairway. "Who doesn't? I know He's up there somewhere, but I've never been able to get a handle on Him."

"Do you go to church?"

"Yes," he said, shaking the ice in his soda glass. "Oh, maybe not all the time after we put the kids through Sunday School." He drained his drink. "Frankly, Marge and I haven't gone that much lately."

"Why not?"

He looked at me quizzically. "You really want to know? I know you go to church regularly, Mike, and I don't want to hurt your feelings. But frankly, I find it boring."

"Why?"

"Oh, I never get much out of it. The minister seems to talk about the same stuff I read in the Philadelphia Inquirer. "So," he shrugged, "why bother?"

I silently prayed for the right words. "Bill, what if I told you there are churches where you'll find the help you need, where the service is so stimulating, so full of life, you won't want it to end?"

He laughed. "Find me a church like that around here and I'll even give up my Sunday morning golf game for it."

Unfortunately, I didn't know of a church in our area that would give Bill what he was searching for. I invited him to the church we were attending but it was too far away for him.

The sad part of it was I met many other men like Bill in our area of northern Philadelphia who were in desperate need of spiritual nourishment, but didn't know where to find it. Frances, my wife, said the same thing about the women she met.

Doctors, lawyers, teachers, computer operators, businessmen and businesswomen, all kinds of people.

"What would you call them?" I asked Fran one day at our lunch table, "Up and outers? They've made it materially, but they're starving."

"Well, you know what they always say, a Christian telling others about the Lord is like a beggar telling other starving beggars where he's found bread."

"But what can we do?" I mused. "Have a Bible study in our home?"

She shook her head. "I don't think it would work."

"Wouldn't it be great," I mused, "if there was a church around here that could give them what they needed?"

Suddenly, the Lord seemed to be tapping me on the shoulder.

I want you and Frances to start a church.

I sat stunned. Us? Begin a new church? Out here in the suburbs?

"Lord," I sighed, "you must have the wrong man. You put me in the automotive parts remanufacturing business, not building churches."

You have been starting churches all the time.

He had me on that one. For years we had started in the plant for ethnic employees, Latinos, Asian, Indian, Portuguese and others who didn't feel comfortable in existing churches. After a church would start on our premises, it would in time grow to where its people obtain their own building on the outside. Eight of these churches were ministering to hundreds of people today.

But begin a church in this suburban area? That's a big order, Lord.

With Me you can do anything.

I could not argue. As I looked back on my life and saw the miracles He had wrought, the impossibilities He had made possible, the healings He had performed, I knew what we had to do.

"Mike?" Frances was regarding me quizzically. "I can tell the Lord has placed something on your heart."

I told her what He had directed.

And thus began a new adventure. It was both exciting and heart breaking. At times we were tempted to give up. Our most tragic moment came when we learned our dear daughter, Ruth, suffered from cancer. We were devastated and could not believe God would take this relatively young woman from her husband, three young children and all of us.

But it was Ruth who helped keep alive our dream for a church.

"Oh Dad, oh Mom," she whispered from her hospital bed, "it sounds so exciting. I can't wait to be there and worship—all of us together."

Sadly, Ruth left us in January 1990 to be with her precious Lord. Fran and I were stricken and, in the agony of our sorrow, starting a new church did not seem very important.

In attempting to make some kind of sense out of Ruth's death, Fran and I found ourselves wondering if there was a connection between God taking her and our vision for a church.

Could it be, we wondered, similar to when Satan went to God about Job and said: "He worships you, but just take away his wealth, and you'll see him curse you to Your face!" Could Satan have said to God: "Just take something precious from those people and see what they will do then about Your church!"

This very thought made us more determined than ever to start His new church. And deep down, Fran and I sensed that our daughter, Ruth, was right there cheering us on.

Now our big question was: Where to start?

We held our first worship service in a place where the early Christians held their meetings: in a house. Our son, Michael and his wife, Jacquie, offered their home and in June 1990 our first service was held with 24 people present. Six of the founding families had made a covenant in prayer and finances to found the new church.

Yet I found myself wondering. Only 24, such a small number. And then I remembered. The first church that started in Jerusalem only had 12.

By the second month, we were running out of room. By August, it had become desperate. Where could we meet?

The Lord answered this one through good food. It so happened one of our vice presidents enjoyed eating at a restaurant in Justa Farm Shopping Center in nearby Huntingdon Valley.

"Mr. Cardone," he said one Monday, "the family and I were eating at DeSumma's restaurant on Sunday and I noticed they had a big banquet room which would be perfect for our church. I talked to the owner and he'd be glad to rent it out Sunday mornings."

So in August of 1990, what we now called the Christian Life Center began meeting in a banquet hall. To me this seemed very fitting. Not only were we offering food for the soul, but so many important Bible events centered around meals. The Passover supper the Jews had the night before God led them out of Egypt, Jesus grilling fish for His disciples on the beach and, of course, the most momentous meal of all, Christ's Holy Communion Supper with His followers on the night before He was crucified.

On that first meeting, our pastor, Reverend Greg Cox spoke on how Christ is our ever present help in trouble. He really reached people, and men like my partner on the golf course, were telling us how much they and their families were being helped. Word spread, and though we were affiliated with the Assemblies of God, it was obvious we were becoming an interdenominational church. We were drawing doctors, realtors, businessmen, construction people, car dealers, accountants, school teachers, men and women of all ages and varying faiths, along with their families.

Soon we had to rent two adjoining stores for church office space as well as room for a youth facility. We expanded to two services to accommodate the crowds and rented a third store for a nursery and children's church. A few months later a fourth store was rented for additional Sunday School facilities.

It appeared we were living up to our name. People were finding new Christian life and seemed to be finding it abundantly.

So much so that by 1991 our worship facilities were so jammed with almost 500 attending, it was clearly evident we had to find larger quarters. The obvious answer was to find a new building large enough, or construct our own church.

Finding a suitable building in the area was impossible. And so began a long search for property on which to build a new House of God. It was heart breaking. If we had wanted to build a new bowling alley, a supper club or cocktail bar, there would be no problem. But a church?

We found plenty of properties but no room for a church. It became obvious that some communities impede zoning for a church because of its non-profit tax basis which does not add to their tax income. It was also clear other communities simply did not want another church.

After being turned down again and again, everywhere we turned, I could not help but think of Jesus' words: "Foxes have dens and birds have nests, but I, the Messiah, have no home of my own–no place to lay my head" (Matthew 8:20 LB).

Would our church ever find a home?

After many frustrating months, I was sitting in my office one morning praying. "Oh Lord, do You really want us to build a church? Please show us where to turn. For we have nowhere to go."

As I prayed, I heard a step at my door and looked up. It was Sam Lepore, one of our long-time supervisors. His face was filled with concern.

"C'mon in, Sam," I said.

I waved him to a chair. "You look like you lost your last friend. What's the problem?"

"It's our church, Mr. Cardone."

I knew Sam was one of the leaders of a small church in Bensalem, a community east of us. I didn't know his church was in a financial bind. As Sam explained it, the bank holding their mortgage wanted to foreclose. Sam said his board felt they had only one hope: a merger of our two churches. "Do you think . . . ," he asked hesitantly, "you folks would be interested?"

I almost heard the angels singing. Here I had been praying only minutes before for some answers to our dilemma and this man comes in with a solution.

"It just might be possible, Sam," I said rising up from my chair, "it just might be . . . " I said in awe, knowing that His Holy Spirit had brought this all about.

Of course, everyone was enthused about the idea. Bensalem's congregation happily became part of the Christian Life Center, we cleared away all mortgage debts, and the result was good news for everybody. When that is the case, you know for sure God is in the arrangement. Bensalem's existing building had a lot of land surrounding it, and it would serve as the nucleus of a new edifice that would rise around it. Architects and construction companies were hired and ground was broken on June 7, 1992 with much prayer.

As construction progressed, Fran and I would often drive out to the site to see what had transpired. One evening as we sat in our car, the sun setting behind the unfinished church, Fran took my hand. "We'll have a nice organ and piano, won't we?"

"Of course, Fran," I said softly, knowing she was thinking of Ruth and how excited she had been about this new house of God. "Ruth will be with us in all our plans." And in a way Ruth was there in the very building of the church. Her son, Eric, took a special interest in its construction and was on the scene overseeing it almost every single day.

Soon the new Christian Life Center on Hulmeville Road in Bensalem began to take shape. The original structure that stood on the grounds was transformed into something entirely new. Now a beautiful building with massive stained glass windows, it was highlighted by a graceful octagonal edifice on one corner with a golden cross soaring to heaven on white winged pinions.

When it was completed, Fran and I walked to its doors emblazoned with a gold cross on a sunburst signifying the resurrection. As we stepped inside, Fran's breath caught. Gleaming organ pipes soared behind the choir loft next to which stood a gracious grand piano. The mahogany pews with off white panels and burgundy carpeting seemed to float in a kaleidoscope glow of colors from the sun streaming through the large stained glass windows.

Out in the foyer a small miracle had taken place. In the original structure, an ugly iron cylinder in the middle of the foyer rose to the ceiling. It was an eyesore and we desperately wanted it removed. But the architects and builders said it had to stay for the column was the central structural support for the building.

Then our gifted interior decorator was blessed with a revelation. "I have an idea," she said, "Let me try it."

More in faith than anything else, we told her to go ahead.

After she finished, Fran and I walked into the foyer and gasped. The once ugly column had been transformed into a magnificent chandelier. Its pink magenta marble base was surmounted by a 24-foot crystal chandelier ablaze with six thousand watts of light and shimmering brass accents bathing the foyer with an incandescent glow.

To me it was a living parable of Christ's transforming grace. Any one of us can be an ugly person like that old iron pole, but Christ can transform us into a being of grace and beauty.

On Easter Sunday of 1993 over 800 people celebrated Christ's resurrection in the new Christian Life Center and it became obvious we would soon have to expand to three services.

On May 9, 1993, the Christian Life Center was dedicated in a beautiful service by Dr. James Kennedy, well-known minister of the Coral Ridge Presbyterian Church in Fort Lauderdale, Florida. Fran played the organ as we all sang "For He is Precious to Me," one of Ruth's favorite hymns which was especially fitting as the church was being dedicated in her memory that day.

As I sat in the congregation with the heavenly music swelling around me I had a vision of an even greater Christian Life Center to come. Here we would soon be reaching 2,500 people in three services. Now I envisioned a new complex on even larger grounds serving at least 10,000 souls with a number of outreach ministries meeting the needs of everyone in the family.

As with Christ's work in us, the Christian Life Center will go on and on. Only God knows the extent of its journey. For we have placed our church as well as ourselves in His hands. In what better place could we be?

The Keys to Success and Happiness

Would you like the same help that guided Michael Cardone in his life?

It's yours for the asking. All you have to do is:

1. Admit that you are a sinner and need to be saved. "For all have sinned, and come short of the glory of God" (Romans 3:23). When we frankly admit this, we've taken the first step.

2. Believe Jesus has provided your salvation. "For God so loved the world, that he gave his only begotten Son, that whosoever believeth in him should not perish, but have everlasting life" (John 3:16). Jesus said, "I am the way, the truth, and the life: no man cometh unto the Father, but by me" (John 14:6).

3. Repent of your sin by turning away from it. "Repent ye therefore, and be converted, that your sins may be blotted out . . ." (Acts 3:19).

4. Accept God's forgiveness. "If we confess our sins, he is faithful and just to forgive us our sins, and to cleanse us from all unrighteousness" (1 John 1:9).

5. Confess. Say aloud what you believe. "If thou shalt confess with thy mouth the Lord Jesus, and shalt believe in thine heart that God hath raised him from the dead, thou shalt be saved" (Romans 10:9).

With Jesus in your heart, you are no longer a slave to worry, fear, and depression. If you let God take over, life will become new and exciting. Jesus said, ". . . I am come that they might have life, and that they might have it more abundantly" (John 10:10). Not only will your life be filled with joy, peace, and happiness, you will also receive the assurance of eternal life through Christ! Jesus said, ". . . He that heareth my word and believeth on him that sent me, hath everlasting life, and shall not come into condemnation; but is passed from death unto life" (John 5:24).

You can receive salvation now by praying this prayer out loud:

Dear God, Your Word shows that I have sinned and need to be saved by Jesus Christ. I repent of my sin and turn to You, Jesus. I believe that You died, were resurrected, and now live. I commit my life to You. Be my Lord and make me a child of God. Father I thank You for my salvation in Jesus' name. Amen.

Rejoice in your new life—a life of "joy unspeakable and full of glory."

If you would like to know more about how God can guide you, write to:

Michael Cardone, Sr.
P.O. Box 5706
Philadelphia, PA 19120-2595

A Biblical Foundation for M. Cardone Ind.

As long as he sought the Lord, God made him to prosper (2 Chronicles 26:5).

* * *

I want the company of the godly men and women in the land; they are the true nobility (Psalms 16:3 TLB).

* * *

The Lord demands fairness in every business deal. He established this principle (Proverbs 16:11 TLB).

* * *

I will bless the Lord who counsels me; he gives me wisdom in the night. He tells me what to do (Psalms 16:7 TLB).

* * *

The master may get better work from an untrained apprentice than from a skilled rebel! (Proverbs 26:10 TLB).

* * *

Commit everything you do to the Lord. Trust him to help you do it and he will (Psalms 37:5 TLB).

* * *

Anyone wanting to be a leader among you must be your servant (Matthew 20:26 TLB).

* * *

Be perfect, be of good comfort, be of one mind, live in peace; and the God of love and peace shall be with you (2 Corinthians 13:11).

* * *

Be strong and courageous and get to work. Don't be frightened by the size of the task, for the Lord my God is with you; he will not forsake you. He will see to it that everything is finished correctly (1 Chronicles 28:20 TLB).

* * *

A sensible man watches for problems ahead and prepares to meet them. The simpleton never looks, and suffers the consequences (Proverbs 27:12 TLB).

* * *

God has given each of us the ability to do certain things well (Romans 12:6 TLB).

* * *

If God has given you administrative ability and put you in charge of the work of others, take the responsibility seriously (Romans 12:8 TLB).

* * *

A lazy fellow is a pain to his employers—like smoke in their eyes or vinegar that sets the teeth on edge (Proverbs 10:26 TLB).

* * *

My protection and success come from God alone. He is my refuge, a Rock where no enemy can reach me (Psalms 62:7 TLB).

* * *

Choose you this day whom ye will serve . . . but as for me and my house, we will serve the Lord (Joshua 24:15).

* * *

Yes, be bold and strong! Banish fear and doubt! For remember, the Lord your God is with you wherever you go (Joshua 1:9 TLB).

* * *

Whatever you wish will happen! And the lights of heaven will shine upon the road ahead of you (Job 22:28 TLB).

* * *

In everything you do, put God first, and he will direct you and crown your efforts with success (Proverbs 3:6 TLB).

M. CARDONE INDUSTRIES, INC.
Statement of Purpose

M. CARDONE INDUSTRIES is a business enterprise. As a business, we realize a profit by meeting the needs of people. Profit permits expansion and strengthening of the business for the benefit of its owners, employees, customers and community. To this end, we pledge ourselves to:

1. HONOR GOD IN ALL WE DO
2. HELP PEOPLE DEVELOP
3. PURSUE EXCELLENCE
4. GROW PROFITABLY

Our business is the Remanufacturing of Automotive Products. Our market is the Automotive Aftermarket.

Our purpose is to:

1. Provide the automotive aftermarket with products of the highest quality, a 100% order fill and the most responsive efficient service available in the industry.

2. Contribute to the conservation of America's natural energy and mineral resources through our recycling of automotive parts.

3. Continually seek ways to offer our customers the greatest potential for profit.

We are an equal opportunity employer seeking to provide for our employees a safe, healthy, comfortable working environment. We encourage a holistic family atmosphere in our working relationships and seek to foster the belief that everyone at M. Cardone Industries is a vital part of a unified, precision team.

M. Cardone Industries is committed to conducting its business relationships in such a manner as to be a credit to God, its owners, our employees, their families, our customers, and the community. Each, though a separate entity, is part of a unified family and the mutual benefit of the whole is achieved as the needs of one another are considered.

Our position is that of a pioneer and proud leader in the automotive remanufacturing industry. We constantly pursue excellence and believe that . . .

"If you want a long and satisfying life . . . never forget to be truthful and kind. If you want favor with both God and man, and a reputation for good judgment and common sense, then trust the Lord completely . . . In everything you do, put God first and He will direct you and crown your efforts with success."

Selections from the Bible:
Proverbs 3
The Living Bible